Cherry

a brownBerry Book

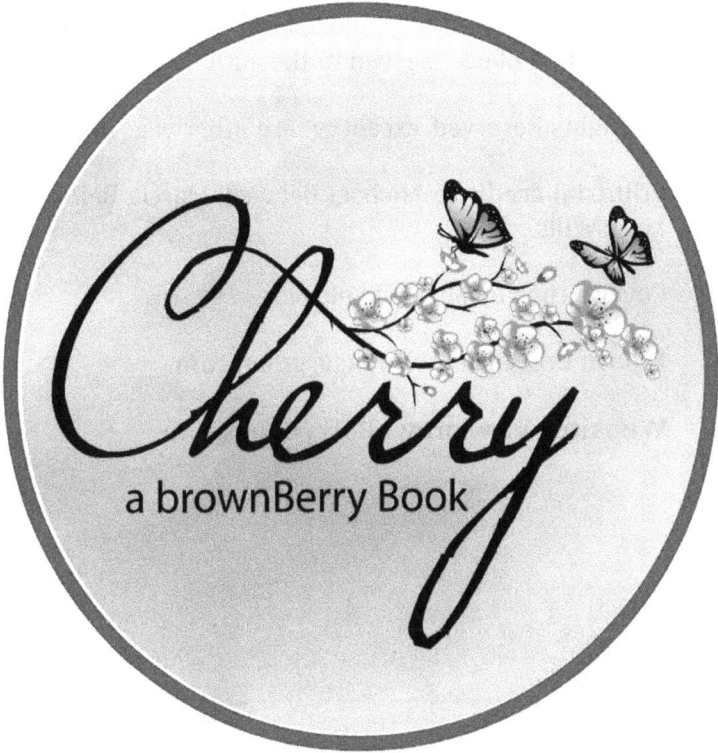

A Personal Growth Compass

BHAKTI MARY

CHERRY

Editorial credit to Michael Beloved, Marcia Beloved and Mark Wills.

Cover design by Michael Beloved.

Email: brownBerryBooks@gmail.com

Website: www.brownBerryBooks.com

We delight in
the beauty of
the butterfly,
but rarely admit
the changes it has
gone through to
achieve that beauty.

Maya Angelou

CHERRY

Contents

CHERRY

Introduction

It is with great humility that I share some of my private thoughts on navigating through life's ups and downs and emerge more beautiful than you ever imagined.

A healthy mind is vital to enduring all that life may present to us. I never imagined the journey that I have traversed and do not know where the road will lead. Choices along the way will be risky but with a firm foundation and knowledge about who I am, I can choose to learn from the outcomes of my choices.

As we watch world events unfold, tragedy is at the center of most that the media covers...unimaginable suffering created by human existence or vast suffering experienced by mankind. As we pause and reflect, it becomes dire that we get our minds in a condition that can endure through and thrive in environments of hardship.

How we treat one another matters but let us begin with how we perceive ourselves. This book focuses on self-health and how to improve our workplace environment.

Dedication

This book is dedicated to my children, Alessandro and Nora. I hope you will find some wisdom in my words. You fill my heart with so much joy and purpose.

A special recognition to my parents, Michael and Marcia, and brother Dear who encouraged me to write and publish. I appreciate you.

Love to my partner, Mark for believing in me and encouraging me. I count on you.

A big hug to Draupadi, Misty, Nicole, Monique, and Bloom who have loved me through everything. You make me better and your support is priceless.

Thank you to every person who ever made a comment on my self-improvement musings and helped me believe that my thoughts were worth reading. Each of you gave me the courage to be vulnerable and to take one more step towards finding and revealing my authentic self.

PART 1

PUTTING POSITIVE IN EACH DAY

Does the thought of putting positive in every day sound overboard? Do you subscribe to the positive thinking movement? There is substantial value in putting positivity in every day. Life is short, and we all deserve better, if not our best, days each and every day. If the ideas I have help you put a little more positive energy into just one more day of your week, then my goal is accomplished.

Focusing on spiritual, mental, and physical fitness is critical to the whole person concept. Physical fitness can result in greater mental agility. In addition to nurturing a healthy lifestyle, we must form the habit of assessing the state of our emotional well-being regularly.

Become aware of the demands or stresses you are facing and how they affect you. Recognize that dedicating time every day to mental fitness will reap significant benefits. It is prudent to schedule mental fitness breaks into your calendar next to every other activity.

Learn to dive into your spiritual nature too, which usually lies buried beneath the myriad of physical, mental and social expression. The most intimate facet of your being, the spiritual nature, will shine through more brightly if you can add even small amounts of "positive" to your mental and physical self.

CHAPTER 1: A Furious Pursuit to Awaken

Once a mother mentioned to me that her son was entering the "why phase". Any parent is intimately familiar with this – where the child is presented with many different thoughts and has the same response of "but why?" I often envy the curiosity and interest of children for it is the emotion that guides their journey through the world and motivates them to learn and explore. The psychologist Sylvan Tomkins explained that "interest is the only emotion that can sustain long-term constructive or creative endeavors." Imagine for a minute if adults had the same level of interest and curiosity as children – if we pursued self-exploration to the point where we knew our own truth.

I furiously long for and pursue my own personal awakening. I would like to think of myself as a seeker but I question and often feel unaware of what to do for this awakening. Right now I am only prepared to awaken on my own terms and conditions. I also realize that the people around me do not wish me to awaken on unknown terms and conditions for fear it will compromise their position in the universe. Perhaps there is a fear that I will be unrecognizable to everyone but myself. It is my challenge to be prepared to do whatever the universe offers me to awaken. I try to live fully in all moments whether they are good or bad.

In my life, the hardest moments have been the most vital to my evolution and progression. Eckhart Tolle reminds us, "Whatever the present moment contains, accept it as if you had chosen it. Always work with it, not against it." He did not recommend that we work with it. No! We are to always work with it and not shy away from it. One of the key things to understand about living in self is that this does not mean to live in one's mind. Rather, it means to be fully present in one's real-life experiences.

Have you ever walked into a store and walked around without knowing what you were looking for? I find myself doing this out of boredom sometimes, but when I think about it, this is the same thing that I do mentally from time to time. It can be referred to as mindless living.

Do not sleep walk through life – this is what you do if you live in your mind where it is easy to disassociate from current circumstances and create imaginary conditions. Even though our reality may be based in our thoughts, we are much more than our thoughts with real-life experiences being where the "rubber meets the road". It is through actual experiences that we exhibit the truth of our being, and others will know who we are.

As I live in my furious pursuit of awakening, you may also wish to join in by asking yourself:

What sparks your awakening daily?

How available and open am I?

What am I searching for?

What do I hope to find?

Am I living an integrated life physically, mentally, emotionally and spiritually?

CHAPTER 2: Being Aware

Mindfulness is a hot topic amongst spiritual leaders, Western philosophers, and psychologists. It is deeply rooted in Buddhist traditions. It is widely used by psychologists to positively alleviate mental and physical conditions.

What is mindfulness and is mindfulness for you?

Marlatt & Kristeller define mindfulness as "bringing one's complete attention to the present experience on a moment-to-moment basis". Jon Kabat-Zinn defines mindfulness as "paying attention in a particular way: on purpose, in the present moment, and non-judgmentally" and as "the art of conscious living". Kabat-Zinn is a prominent teacher of mindfulness meditation and the founder of the Mindfulness-Based Stress Reduction program at the University of Massachusetts Medical Center. He is sometimes referred to as the father of modern mindfulness.

Mindfulness for Beginners by Kabat-Zinn is a good primer for understanding this basic idea that is being studied in depth by many of our respected philosophers and spiritual leaders and reported to help children and adults in EVERY aspect of their lives. Mindfulness is for everyone!

One idea that caught me by surprise in Kabat-Zinn's book was the concept of adjusting one's default setting. The state of thinking is our default setting. Mindfulness emphasizes being aware over being lost in thought. I had never really thought about how much time I spend thinking when I could be enjoying the present moment.

Throughout the day, I am physically present but mentally absent and disengaged during many experiences. Kabat-Zinn compares thoughts to the commentary one hears during a sporting event. The commentary reflects someone else's views and opinions of the event. The sporting event would be viewed and experienced differently without the commentary.

I remember attending my first National Football League game where the Cincinnati Bengals played. I found myself bored at the game. Instead of delving into all the statistics and random facts about the players and teams that are normally highlighted by the sportscasters, I found myself surrounded by the dialogue of deaf fans and the faint call for each play on the field. I couldn't even make out the players on the field from my cheap nosebleed seats.

Thoughts are the self-generated voice-over of life. Mostly these thoughts are about the past or future. Kabat-Zinn says that "thinking completely dominates our lives and colors everything we feel and do and care about". Sometimes, it is the continuous negative thought pattern reel. What if we silenced the outside and inside voices once in a while? Life could be experienced differently with an increased focus on being aware of the here and now without the often annoying, negative, and destructive voice-over. Think – is your mind full of cluttered commentary OR are you aware and mindful of the present experience?

The essence of mindfulness is noticing when we are lost in thoughts and being aware enough to deliberately return to the present experience.

Mindfulness is being instead of doing; it is being present now. I often spend my work day multi-tasking over ten tasks at a time. I bounce from one task to another all day and sometimes, I do not complete any task. Social and family obligations are mixed in with work tasks and the to-do list never gets shorter.

The state of doing is the mindless rush and the non-stop juggling of all aspects of our life all day every day. The state of being is being present for the moment of right now. It is forgetting about the to-do-list long enough to focus on a singular task or moment in front of us.

Just BE.

BE aware.

CHAPTER 3: Love Is All Around

I was watching an older film called *Love Actually*, and a quote stuck with me — "If you look for it, I've got a sneaky feeling you'll find that love actually is all around." I began to think about whether this was actually true. The movie inferred that love did not have to be pointed directly at us to be experienced.

In 2015, I took a trip with my fiancé Mark to Budapest, Hungary. On the same trip, we decided to travel to Sheffield, England where my great uncle Ivelaw Walker had migrated to in the 1960s from Guyana. Here, he and his wife Sheila raised a large family so I met over 30 cousins for the first time. I appreciated this trip because it redefined my viewpoint of relationships. In this family, there were many relationships that were incredibly loving but not bound by marriage and I had been feeling pressure to abide by the American tradition of marriage in my relationship with Mark. In England, there was not that pressure — what I did find were relationships founded on trust. My great aunt trusted that the father of her then first child would send for her as he had promised when he set sail from Guyana to England and a year later after he worked in England and saved some money, he did send for her and their child. Traditions are just that – traditions but they are not binding – there are no such limitations, boundaries or boxes that can be placed upon or around you unless you let it happen to you. Stop letting things happen to you.

Love knows no boundaries. It surrounds us unconditionally in ways that defy imagination. It is our minds that create limits on love.

I experienced something else very positive in that trip to Sheffield. In most conversations with family and strangers alike, sentences ended in words of endearment such as "love" or "dear" or "sweetheart" or "darling". I found that the simple and regular use of these terms of endearment completely and positively changed my opinion of the interaction and my subsequent response.

We can substantially benefit from being casual observers of love. If we can become aware of the acts of love happening all around us, we could become more loving ourselves. What do you think? Is there some merit to this thought?

Some ways that love is expressed around you are through expressions of affection, gratitude, kindness, generosity, and forgiveness. Make a habit of smiling when you recognize love and deliberately generate a subsequent corresponding act of love. Love can be a lifelong experience involving everything around you.

At a basic level and with utmost respect and recognition of humanity, love is not just reserved for our children, spouses, family, and friends. Too often, we think if we are not getting love from the ONE person that matters most to us (a spouse, child, sibling, parent, friend), then we are not loved and there is no love. However, once we learn to recognize the signs and expressions of love all around us, we can move from being a casual observer to being a participant. We can also expand our sources of love from sources closest to us to sources all around us.

I find it fascinating that we often expect all of our support and needs to be met by one person – usually our spouse or significant other. By expanding our sources of love, we can relieve the burden of unreasonable expectation from family. We can allow each other to fully participate in experiences such as parenting and not feel as if we (the adults) have been robbed of our significant other's attention when it is the child whose foundation is shaky and whose future relies on their parent's full love. This mindset may result in happier relationships that bear fruit we never imagined.

How can we further expand our participation in love? It is the ultimate form of love to believe in others' potential, celebrate their successes, be their advocates and to treat them with kindness.

We can only consistently do this by making a deliberate effort to remove our anxieties, resentments and stresses so we do not consciously or unconsciously pass them on to others.

We must also remove the preconception that everyone must change themselves to come into alignment with our personal preferences. Why do we have to look at people with the idea that they need to change SOMETHING or that they always need to agree with us on everything? Will you be personally affected if most people change nothing at all around you or would both parties be happier in the presence of genuine acceptance?

Are you able to let others voice their opinions without you feeling less than? Most of the time, people do not tell us we are "less than" – *we FEEL that and then project it onto others as if they told us that*.

How can you authentically illuminate others? Well, you must truly believe that your encounters with others are love personified or a call for love. If you are looking for love, you will discover that love is all around. When you recognize it, you become connected to it. Let love be your connection to the universe in its authentic state.

CHAPTER 4: Finding Beauty Everywhere

Once, I took my son to a local park with a good friend and her two sons. I was pleased to see such a stunning variety of trees and wildflowers. As we admired the beautiful flowers there and as I took pictures of all the flowers with my cell phone, my son told me I should send the pictures to my mother and my sisters. Upon further thought, he decided I should send them to all my female friends and family. What a considerate child! I decided to post them on my online blog so that everyone could see them. Later I expanded my distribution via social media and called it "visual candy".

Looking at beauty in the world, is the
first step of purifying the mind.

— Amit Ray —

Naturally occurring "visual candy" is a free and readily available source of gratitude. It is free and readily available. You can substitute it for other unhealthy things that make you feel good in the short-term but then come back to bite. Use the beauty in nature as a well spring for positive inspiration.

When you slow down and when you are present, you cannot help but notice that there is astonishing beauty everywhere. For me, spring and summer are the times of year when I experience the most beautiful colors and visual inspirations. At the beginning and end of most days, there is the sunrise and sunset...and, as you go about the day, beauty is certain to be expressing itself in discreet or obvious ways. When you begin to see this, be aware of the natural gratitude that awakens within. Use this to propel yourself into positive interactions with others.

CHAPTER 5: Find Gratitude Now

Do you notice all the little things in your life or do they pass you by? Did you notice the world around you today?

Do you walk through life in a daze feeling overwhelmed, lethargic, entitled, dissatisfied, unrecognized, or under achieving? Is your daily dialogue centered around negative energy and things you do not like? Do you only celebrate the big stuff? Are you chasing the next thing or the same thing in perpetuity?

Is there anything "small" for which you are grateful? Can you find a reason to celebrate right now?

There are 86,400 seconds in one day. How many of those have you used to say "Thank You" or to express gratitude?

The first step to gratitude is being present and aware. Being present allows you to experience a recurring colorful touch by life. If you are in a daze, you are unable to acknowledge or

27

appreciate the small pop-up things or the recurring things that are just always there.

It is time to wake up. Suman Rai says:

"Choose happiness today by taking life moment by moment, complaining very little, and being thankful for the little things that mean a lot".

I challenge you to stop and take time today to appreciate the small things and moments that are positively contributing to your life. Count your blessings! Start by appreciating the opportunity to read and browse on the Internet.
One-third of the world has no access to the Internet and over 700 million people in the world cannot read. Now, take 5-10 minutes to write a list of 15 things you are grateful for. Here's mine:

1. I am grateful for the job I have.

2. I am grateful for a comfortable place to stay.

3. I am grateful for food to eat and water to drink.

4.   I am grateful for the skill of writing and typing.

5.   I am grateful for family and friends.

6.   I am grateful for my struggles which have made me the person I am today.

7.   I am grateful for curiosity and the desire to learn.

8.   I am grateful for my current healthy existence.

9.   I am grateful for innovation.

10. I am grateful for diversity and uniqueness.

11. I am grateful for the beauty in nature.

12. I am grateful for my sight, hearing, and touch.

13. I am grateful to everyone who has taught me and loved me.

14. I am grateful for laughter and smiles.

15. I am grateful for today.

Take your list and put it in a place you regularly frequent. Revisit it when you are feeling down or dazed. Add to it, too!

CHAPTER 6: Five Simple Ways to Put Positive Everywhere

Do you need daily reminders to be positive? Think about the places you go every day and add built-in positive reminders. If you increase your positive thinking, I believe positive actions are not far behind.

Keep your thoughts positive because your thoughts become your words.

Keep your words positive because your words become your behavior.

Keep your behavior positive because your behavior becomes your habits.

Keep your habits positive because your habits become your values.

Keep your values positive because your values become your destiny.

— Ghandi —

Sometimes all it takes is a simple reminder to get you back on the track of positive thinking. If others happen to see your reminder, maybe it will help them too. The concept here is to create passive and inconspicuous ways to reset or redirect your behavioral patterns.

Here are five simple ideas for putting positive reminders around you:

1) You may get in your CAR at least twice daily. Get custom positive plates or a key chain.

2) You probably visit your BATHROOM multiple times each day. Put a positive decoration in your bathroom or near your sink. Vinyl decals are a nice low-cost addition to any wall or mirror.

3) You may sit at your WORK DESK for 8+ hours a day. Put some positive décor on computer desktop or desk.

4) You probably type multiple PASSWORDS each day. Use a positive password for a positive nudge upon use.

5) You may look at your PHONE dozens of times each day. Put an uplifting background on your

home screen and screen saver. Try getting a phone case with an uplifting message.

CHAPTER 7: The Importance of Having a Belief System

When my son was a toddler, my father strongly advised me to bring him up with some religion. He emphasized that it did not matter which one as long as there was one – one that gave him something to believe in. I think what he meant was to raise him with a belief system.

The concepts I discuss are generally religion neutral. While religions can certainly inform one's belief system, it is not necessary to be a part of a specific religion to have a robust and healthy belief system.

A belief system is what supports you and gives you comfort; it is your belief of how you fit into the universe. It is a great benefit that you do not have to prove your belief system to anyone. You do not have to justify it either. A personal belief system requires no template because it is tailored to you. By using a steering mechanism as a comparison, we can see that a belief system is the steering wheel plus all the software and hardware behind it. Occasionally, you may wish to upgrade, personalize, or customize your software and hardware. Then, all you must do is turn. If you find yourself turning in the wrong direction, just make a correction; some corrections may be slight or gradual and some may be very sudden and pronounced.

A robust belief system skillfully steers you through your actions and reactions. At the core of my belief system is compassion and the golden rule. What is at the core of yours?

CHAPTER 8: Avoiding Anger and Blame

There are opportunities in everyday life to self-correct, self-reflect, and self-analyze. In the course of our interactions, we either continue to affirm our core beliefs or we adjust them. I once advised an old friend to remember that negativity is almost never rewarded. This particular friend has ended up in a rather precarious situation with his professional career that was derailing the life he had envisioned.

Nothing is permanent...neither success nor failure. He went from being a skilled electrical and computer engineer to being under investigation by the federal government. While I will refrain from offering details, I understood that despite carrying out the process of fighting for his self-proclaimed innocence, the outcome may still be beyond his control. That potential always exists.

We wishfully think we are in control of something, yet we discover that we cannot willfully control everything. We think we could have changed something, but life moves on without us while we wallow in the sorrows of "what ifs" and "whys". Often times, we find ourselves in circumstances where a negative response and outlook seem to be the only option. I would offer that this is NEVER the ONLY option.

When an outcome is not what we planned and worked for we do not have to assign blame, determine why, or angrily cast negativity on ourselves or others.

Take pause to determine if the anger you harbor or the blame you place has the potential to benefit you or anyone else. Avoid fruitless anger and blame at all cost.

— Bhakti Mary —

We can always choose to not assign blame and to not buy into the negativity produced by assigning blame to all parts of our lives that do not go as we envisioned or planned. We can always choose to keep our heads up, to keep pressing past the disappointments and to keep pressing past the consequences we consistently experience because of our choices. We can keep learning and keep climbing out of the valleys. We can let go!

The old friend responded that he would do his best to take a page out of my book and be positive. And he added faith and trust in God to this. "To my book?", I asked. He said, "Your playbook. It is an expression. You are so good at being positive and not getting angry even when others deserve it." It would take 19 months for his name to get cleared of the charges and, during this time, he lost his job and his position as a graduate student. I do not know how he rebounded from this experience, but I can only hope that his experience did not leave him raw, bitter and vengeful.

At the end of the day, you must have a clear understanding of your own belief system, what you desire to gain through it, and, even more importantly, to know what the outputs of such a system are likely to be. You have to keep trying, keep adjusting and morphing, and keep moving! Do not get stuck in a rut!

Now, I am not perfect. I also feel negative at times and reactionary instead of visionary, but I try to remind myself to steer clear of the "doom and gloom" mindset (a negative and counterproductive thought pattern). Sharing this with you allows me to verbalize the affirmations herein and to keep trying.

As I advise you, so I advise and remind myself. Keep your head up. Be prepared to face life no matter what it brings to you and try to react without feelings of entitlement, anger, blame, and ultimately negativity. You can survive anything and still emerge with hope and optimism from the gravest of circumstances but ONLY by doing your best to maintain a positive outlook.

CHAPTER 9: Rise and Shine!

I used to wake my son up in the morning with an energetic and fairly loud "Rise and Shine" in the hopes that he would jump out of bed enthusiastically ready for the day. What usually happened is that he would roll over slowly, peek from under the covers with a squinty-eyed scowl and ask if he can sleep at least five more minutes. How do you wake up in the morning? Is it with a *Rise and Shine* or *Rise and Whine* mentality?

As adults, our wake up routine can be far more calculated than the wake up routine of a child. How can we get from rising to shining? I offer to you that personal vectoring can help tremendously. What is personal vectoring? Personal vectoring is self-dialogue intended to carry you in a specific direction. A few years ago, I started a practice of saying a silent prayer or statement of intention prior to opening my eyes.

It goes something like this: "Thank you for allowing me to rise and see another day. Thank you for the blessings you have granted me throughout my life. Thank you for the opportunities this day will offer. Help me to say positive things to people. Help me to smile and acknowledge people. Help me to be productive and open to learning. Help me to listen better and to be energetic. Help me to be progressive – to be part of solutions. Help me let go of negativity. Help me to stay focused."

This self-dialogue goes on for one to three minutes. Then, I open my eyes and go about my day. Does it help me? It certainly cannot hurt. My days do not always go as planned but often this self-dialogue follows me throughout the day as I interact with others and choose my reactions to my dynamic environment. While my actions are not always perfect, I have become more aware of my surroundings and my reactions and I find it easier to identify where improvement is warranted.

I believe that starting the day with statements of intention represents a fruitful examination and acknowledgement of self. Acknowledgement of our existence and associated gratitude as well as recognition of areas requiring improvement is healthy. It does not have to be said aloud. I doubt my significant other who sleeps next to me has any knowledge of this inner dialogue. Nor does he need to! Next time you wake up, try these five simple steps:

1. Recite a personal statement. (who are you?)
2. Recite at least 3 statements of intention. (see Make Compassion Your Simple Religion section)
3. Smile.
4. Rise and SHINE!
5. Be your best self. (action beats intention every time)

CHAPTER 10: Does Negativity Weaken You Too?

Can a relationship last when the negative-to-positive ratio is imbalanced? This condition exists when one person is significantly more negative in their mentality than the other person. What happens when someone's relationship is at stake due to this imbalance? Can a person actually change from the "glass half empty" to the "glass half full" mentality?

But misery loves company, you say! Well, I say, misery hates my company, so does toxicity. I choose not to prolong a self-induced struggle every day. I am working to choose not to be so susceptible to the weakening energy of other people's negativity. Even if we master this, we can still be affected by the negativity of others.

Sometimes I feel that some of the people closest to me are in a perpetual state of helplessness. Their concentration on the bad parts of everything causes cynicism, pessimism, emotional instability and depression not only for themselves but for the people they encounter.

To take it one step further, toxicity is when you are dealing with a person who primarily sees the glass as empty when one thing happens they do not like...the 'doom and gloom' mentality.

I am simply not the type to complain about everything, criticize everyone or see the bad side of everything. I am extremely sensitive to the emotions of others and I am very aware of them. For me, and I am sure I am not alone, the negative moods of others exhausts me. I have yet to develop the proper mechanism to prevent this emotional and physical draining. It takes me to a place so far from my center that I feel an urge to run far away from its source. I have reached a stage in my life where I am truly fed up with the obsession and focus our society places on negativity as if it is the majority of activity and as if it is truly productive. The resultant state of paranoia, fear and negativity in many people is disturbing.

Most people get angry, bothered, or upset by things they cannot change. Their negative reactions change nothing outside of their own body. In fact, people often react to negativity with negativity. It is a vicious circle. The impact of stress and negativity on our bodies is also far from positive. Next time you feel yourself being negative, try to find the love around you.

For those of us struggling to stay positive because of the negativity around us, one key realization is clearly understanding that our job is not to help people overcome their negativity. Our role is to focus within ourselves and figure out how to be unaffected or how to minimize the impact or response.

So back to the original questions:

Can a relationship last when the negative-to-positive ratio is imbalanced? Yes, if one person learns to handle the negativity better. We cannot survive if we are consistently feeding off of one another's negativity. Perhaps, a positive side effect of this approach is that the other person can over time see the benefits of positivity!

What happens when someone's relationship is at stake due to this imbalance? The relationship must be important enough to induce mindful change on both sides. We cannot underestimate the impact of our own negativity on others. On the other side, we cannot underestimate the impact of deliberately managing our response to the negativity of others.

Can a person actually change from the "glass half empty" to the "glass half full" mentality? Maybe. It is up to that person to find the love around themselves and cultivate it within.

CHAPTER 11: Intentions and Actions

As you go throughout your day, what if you had to speak aloud your intention for each action?

Do you dislike your intentions? Do your intentions disappoint or embarrass you? Would they disappoint others?

Do your actions actually align with your intentions? Are your actions for the benefit of all? I encourage you to be clear with yourself about your intentions. Then, remember actions always beat intentions.

Now, we can all probably say and reasonably justify to ourselves that all of our actions serve (or at some time) served a positive purpose. Remember that your intentions should aid you in taking greater control of your life.

Without intention, you may stray anywhere. If your actions do not seem to reflect your intentions, I encourage you to find new actions that successfully achieve the positive intentions.

Your truth is reflected in your actions. Be aware of your actions and acknowledge the intentions behind your actions. Try to align your actions and intentions. Write down your intentions and demonstrate your commitment to act in alignment with your intentions.

Is there noticeable change in your behavior over time or have you been stagnant? Use examination of self to shed light on your truths and aim to be better than you have ever been. Aim to be your very best!

CHAPTER 12: Be Genuine and Act

Several years ago, I was at a local grocery store and had a full cart of food. I was checking out when I noticed the man behind me. He didn't wear fancy clothing and didn't look clean. He had a small basket with about 10 Hungry Man frozen meals and a few other items.

I had a strange feeling inside and told the cashier to add his groceries to my bill. She relayed the news to him and his demeanor immediately changed. A small smile appeared on his face as he asked "Are you sure?" I said "I am 100% sure. Please allow me to pay for your items sir".

His smile grew bigger and tears appeared in his tired eyes. "Thank you. You have given me hope in the good of people again. No one has ever done anything like this for me before", he said. I gave a warm smile, told him I was glad to help, and wished him a good evening.

As I went to my new truck in the parking lot, I watched the man walk to his vehicle — a very old one with plastic duct taped in the place of some windows. He needed grace. And I needed to be reminded that I would never have so much as to prevent me from lending a helping hand or demonstrating the essence and purpose of humanity – COMPASSION.

If you think you are so far above the homeless or the people who have less than you financially, mentally, emotionally, spiritually, etc., you might find yourself in their position sooner than later so you can in fact discover how close you are.

We cannot seek or attain health, wealth, learning, justice or kindness in general. Action is always specific, concrete, individualized, and unique.

— Benjamin Jowett —

Most days we utter generic words of our great intentions. We are all in varying positions in and through which we can make a difference in people's lives. Kindness does change people. It is not a sign of weakness. You can restore one's hope in humanity or have a powerful impact that they remember for the rest of their life.

Instead of being generic about your intentions, be genuine and ACT. Here are ten ways to keep kindness going and to be genuine.

1. Thank a veteran when you see one. The same goes for any profession. Take opportunities to communicate how you value others for their services.

2. Buy a meal for someone at another table when you go out to eat.

3. Smile at others. Even If they do not smile back, they will be taken to a happy place from your smile alone.

4. Choose to be patient with retail employees. Do not be the normal rude customer that they encounter regularly.

5. Volunteer! Services that help those in need often only exist because of volunteers.

6. Utter a simple "good morning" with a smile as you run into people in the morning. Set the tone for a great day.

7. Pay compliments. Many people think nice things about people but never utter them.

8. Adopt a family in need during the holidays. This is an experience you will never forget – putting a smile on the face of parents and children during a holiday is truly rewarding.

9. Exercise patience in situations where you find yourself waiting. This is an opportunity to stop and think – to settle down mentally and to reset! Take it.

10. Send a random card to family. Let them know you love them. Some family always wonders if anyone truly cares about them. Though they may never express this, they do wonder – trust me! Send something and remove the doubt.

Goethe said:

"Kindness is the golden chain by which society is bound together".

I believe this to be true. Through kindness and compassion, we are all connected. When we act kindly and feel kindly towards others, we develop a certain inner happiness and peace. Living in self allows us to be at peace with our surroundings. Too often we underestimate the power of kindness and caring. It can create the hope we have all been waiting for!

CHAPTER 13: Finding Infinite Levels of Success

June 2, 2014 marked the 10th anniversary of my graduation from the United States Air Force Academy, and I could not help but think as I read classmates' anniversary Facebook posts how proud they all must be of this accomplishment. For some, this was the biggest moment of their life! How can we remain proud or maintain a strong self-esteem after such an experience?

Most people I encounter are not aware of this accomplishment of mine, and it will have little meaning for them if I conduct myself disrespectfully. You might be thinking that pride is a bad thing, but someone once told me that pride is the virtue of respecting oneself.

Pride is a rational evaluation of self where one has done something worthy of the praise received. Here's where it gets real! A proud person often wants to continuously improve him or herself. My personal desire to improve myself motivated and propelled me to write this book. I advise you not to measure achievements against anyone else's achievements; this would be being prideful. I want you to be proud of who you are, so I encourage you to "give it 100" and give life your best, not someone else's best.

Let me offer an honest thought: Sometimes, I take for granted things that happen on a daily basis that are both ordinary and extraordinary and forget the value of experiences that I have accomplished. Sometimes, my gratitude is lacking.

In daily moments of gratitude, we pause to witness infinite levels of success in ourselves and others.

— Bhakti Mary —

While we should remember the past and be proud of experiences like a college graduation, we should also look to the present for moments to be proud of. With a sense of humility, take a look around and discover or recollect what and who you can be proud of in all dimensions of your life. Live inside out.

Here are 5 tips for staying proud in the present:

1. TAKE CARE OF YOUR BODY. Eat healthy, sleep plenty, and exercise regularly. Always dress like you matter. Develop and test your endurance and discipline.

2. BE UPLIFTING. Steer clear of negative, energy-depleting people. Surround yourself with positive people. Use social media in a productive manner to uplift yourself and others.

3. STAY COMMITTED TO THE EXPERIENCE CALLED LIFE. Approach life with joy. Start by being open and friendly. Say, "Hello, how are you?" to friends, family and strangers. Reach out. Be willing to lighten someone else's load. If someone needs help, be there. Speak up for the timid. Show them you have noticed their plight. Spend quality time with people. Share, learn and laugh.

4. TAKE CARE OF YOUR MIND. Always participate in continuous learning opportunities. This could be anything that increases your knowledge foundation such as enrolling in classes and

reading current events. Affirm yourself. Recite your personal statement regularly. Stop the negative thought patterns. Recharge self. Be still. Be quiet. Be aware. Reflect. Awaken.

5. RECOGNIZE YOURSELF AND OTHERS. Watch success. Success is happening all around you. Acknowledge it – all of it. Own your failures. A failure or mistake is a learning experience – a lesson. Forgive self and others for failures. Do not harbor resentments. Learn and progress.

CHAPTER 14: Breaking the Cycle of Making Excuses

What is an excuse? Excuses are mechanisms to help us feel better about behaviors we need to justify, mechanisms to avoid the truth, mechanisms to avoid scrutiny, mechanisms to self-preserve while self- destructing, mechanisms to avoid situations and to relieve us of the calling to lead a responsible life and attain goals, mechanisms to tell lies and live lies, mechanisms to temporarily boost our ego by inflating our worthiness in the eyes of others while deflating personal self-worth, mechanisms to hide shortcomings, and mechanisms to put our failures in a better light.

How can we recognize habitual excuse makers? Are you one? Think of the people in your life who always have a reason (a self-rationalized "excuse") for why they are not succeeding or who always have a reason for why their life is subpar today. No one likes a habitual excuse maker. We all make excuses, but think of people who consistently find ways to psychologically and emotionally hide failure and to resist accepting defeat and taking responsibility for their actions.

Habitual excuse makers define themselves by the excuses they make about why they cannot be who they want to be or do what they truly want to do. They believe that instead of working hard, they can make excuses for not working at all or working at suboptimal levels.

Being an excuse maker can be difficult to change if it has become a way of life. What should you do if you are a habitual excuse maker?

He that is good for making excuses is seldom good for anything else.

— Benjamin Franklin —

While it is easier to make excuses about circumstances rather than actually doing anything about them, part of growing up involves taking responsibility for our actions and imperfections and admitting our failures.

We must not ignore our current state or deny it — we should instead be honest about it and acknowledge it for what it is.

The immature person makes excuses to avoid the responsibility of his own potential.

— Wade Sadlier —

Taking responsibility for actions and associated outcomes means entertaining the notion that you might need to rethink how you go about your life. Are you open to the possibility of necessary wholesale changes in certain parts of your life or do you tend to hide behind facades of excuses to shield you from personal guilt? Jordan Belfort says that "The only thing standing between you and your goal is the bullshit story you keep telling yourself as to why you cannot achieve it." What is the story? It is the excuse.

Do you accept performance or do you accept excuses? Be humble and open to becoming profoundly aware of your shortcomings so that you might be in a better position to achieve your full potential.

Develop performance goals and develop sustained momentum to reaching those goals through execution of action plans. Do whatever it takes! Invest in yourself, and push beyond your limits. To succeed, we must be ready to make the change, believe in ourselves, and be willing to move. Sometimes we can't do it alone and that's ok; get the support you need to depart from your comfort zone.

Be ready to make the change. Most people are not ready to do the work required to change. People resist change, yet change is the only constant in life. When your life becomes so intolerable that you realize that the only way to overcome your reality is to move through and beyond each experience, then you will change. In the meantime while you continue to self-perpetuate the excuse of "I'm not ready", do not expect friends to listen to or give credence to your made up story.

Believe in yourself. Most people do not believe in themselves. They also hide shamefully behind their feelings of self-doubt. If you do not believe in yourself, do not expect friends to indefinitely believe in you. Eventually they will realize that their belief will not matter because you are not ready to do the work required to establish your own belief in self. Become self-reliant and trust and believe in yourself. You have the right to live your life as you envision it, and you concurrently have the right and responsibility to own your successes, failures and excuse-filled stories.

Be willing to move. Most people continue doing what they know. They are stuck in a place they think is comfortable because they are afraid to be vulnerable and to grow in a new situation. When others realize that you are no longer relevant in your comfort zone, you will be moved forcefully due to irrelevance. Before this happens, stretch out of the zone and maneuver through the unknown – have an exciting life NOW. It's never as bad as it seems.

Also, do not expect to be recognized in your stagnant comfort zone. Use the tools from your new experiences to continue propelling you forward into areas where you feel stronger, more confident and more capable than you ever realized possible.

What should you do if you are friends with a habitual excuse maker? Discontinue the bad habit of making excuses for people's excuses. Do not accept or tolerate people's poor behavior and actions that are primarily intentional and within their control. Surround yourself with quality people. John Wooden said, "Never make excuses. Your friends do not need them and your foes won't believe them." He was right – friends do not let friends make excuses and they do not listen to bullshit stories over and over.

What do friends do for friends? Friends encourage development of clarity, confidence, courage and commitment. Friends encourage you to become committed to changing and they hold you accountable when you make excuses. Friends encourage friends to be clear about their life instead of living in a haze of excuses. Friends encourage friends to be confident and to find self-worth based on reality not a self-worth rooted lies and excuses. Having this commitment and clarity is key to establishing the confidence and courage necessary to plunge out of the comfort zone into a world full of possibilities where our potential can be tapped.

CHAPTER 15: Unwrapping The Gift

Each day is a brand new gift. Wake up and take the gift wrap off. Look inside and embrace the opportunities. Start by simply taking credit and responsibility for the choices that you make. Choose letting go over anger, counting blessings over envy, and getting up over giving up. Choices matter. Healthy choices matter. Be determined to rise above self-pity.

See yourself and take time to examine yourself. Harness your inner strength to persevere through the day – know that things won't be easy but you should be determined to never give up no matter how long it takes to reach your goals. Never give up! While you are persevering, take a minute to stop looking for fulfillment in your future – do not miss the present moment in your pursuit for "greener grass".

In the present, focus on what is important. Take the pressure off the urgent tasks and focus on the important things. The book *The One Thing* is an excellent read to help you understand how to maneuver successfully and less chaotically through the rat race. Some days, put down the long to-do-list that never seems to go away, and stop the monotonous way you routinely traverse through the day in. Live in the present moment. Make life count.

CHAPTER 16: Bringing Light to Others

I was once presented with the proposition with a coworker and friend. Often myself and two female co-workers enjoyed going out for movies, dinner or even happy hour after work. One co-worker then suggested that one Sunday, we could volunteer together. I happily accepted the invitation. A lot of people steer away from volunteering because they prefer not to work for free unless the benefit is personal. I enjoy helping others and so we volunteered five hours on a Sunday to prepare and serve meals to whoever wanted to come for a free hot meal at the *House of Bread* in Dayton, Ohio.

First things first, when you volunteer to do something, people are counting on you and it is important to be dependable. We showed up on time as promised!

I did not know what to expect but I was determined to be enthusiastic and open minded. I was open to doing anything I was asked to do and requested work when I was not busy so as to be a good teammate. The *House of Bread* serves a hot meal 365 days a year and it is through the cooperation of volunteers that this is possible. The meal for that day was chicken, rice soup, squash, asparagus with mushrooms, fruit, bread, and dessert. Guests were also offered milk, water and coffee.

Through this experience, I was not only exposed to different kinds of people but I was also exposed to a different side of my friends. I was able to see them in a new light. I now respect and look up to them even more, and I know that we are people with similar souls. I was also challenged to interact with the rest of the volunteers so my social confidence increased as the day passed.

I learned that even if I did not know what to do, someone would help me. The funny part was that one of my friends had never cooked a meal in her life. She was blessed (most women would say) to have a husband that had cooked every meal over the past 20 years. This did not shy her away from volunteering at this kitchen though. We joked that the people would never return to the kitchen if she did cook. Thankfully (I joke) and ironically, she didn't cook at this kitchen either.

Being in the *House of Bread* allowed me to reflect on my life and to observe other peoples' realities. Seeing this contrast of my life to theirs reminded me to appreciate my life more and reminded me of the value of empathy to those who are seemingly less fortunate. I tried to view the world through their eyes and to imagine their experience. It humbled me.

I was humbled as older people came through the line and were delighted to receive the meal. I was further humbled as young parents brought their children through the line in their Sunday best. While these people may have been in an unhappy state of their life, for the most part, being able to eat a hot meal made them just a bit happier. I realized that my attitude was critical and I decided to immerse myself in the experience.

When interacting with people who were my elders and people who were my age and younger, I was respectful but delightful and friendly. Being the person serving the dessert, I was quite popular! I smiled and showed them that I was at the kitchen because I wanted to be there with them serving them. It is important to be respectful of people, even those who are struggling; if you were in that position, you would be grateful if other humans respected you and treated you with decency.

Throughout my five hours at the *House of Bread* in Dayton, Ohio, I also observed that the leadership was very enthusiastic yet disciplined. Their verbal and nonverbal cues demonstrated that they wanted to be there with us for the purpose of serving a hot, nutritious, lunchtime meal to anyone in need. Their positive attitudes and guidance allowed complete strangers to work together to achieve a goal of serving a hot meal at a specific time to several hundred people who needed it. This impressed on me the value of being as a leader what you wish to see in your followers. This was an excellent "leadership by example" laboratory.

At the end of the meal, we were then asked to partake in some of the leftovers. I took the opportunity to sample the foods we had cooked and sat in the chairs that the needy had sat in. Here I reflected on their experience. Some of the needy still sat in the facility consuming the last bits of their meal too. Next, we were asked to clean the facility. Me and my friends cleaned tables, stacked chairs, swept floors, and mopped floors. It was important to finish the job. In order to serve the meal the next day on time, the facility had to be cleaned that day.

I was very thankful for the reminder the five hours provided me: I am human. We are all human. It is my responsibility to be compassionate. Compassion is my religion. Only by immersing myself in different realities can I provide myself with the contrast necessary for gratefulness. It is in these realities that one's true character is revealed and refined. Do not be afraid. Dive into someone else's world. Your 5 hours matter!

What is a volunteer experience you enjoyed and what did it teach you?

CHAPTER 17: Making Compassion Your Simple Religion

Do you want to bring immediate and long term happiness to your life? I am sure you answered yes! Then, it is time to start cultivating and practicing compassion daily — make compassion your simple religion. I believe that acts of compassion can improve our health, well-being, and relationships with everyone — strangers, friends, family, spouses, and children.

Compassion is unconditionally caring about people's happiness as if it were your own and seeking to increase it without reward. It is a sense of shared suffering combined with a desire to reduce the suffering of others. It is the Golden Rule's action verb! The first place we learn how to live with other people is at home — the home is the school of compassion and the family are the students. One of the most important things we can teach our children is the lesson of compassion — compassion is a way of life!

Many of us are familiar with suffering because it is the part of the human experience that bonds us all together. What is suffering? It is that which causes pain. First, look in self. Then, look around you.

"Look into your own heart, discover what it is that gives you pain and then refuse, under any circumstance whatsoever, to inflict that pain on anybody else."

— Karen Armstrong —

Tune into others in a kind and loving manner. Compassion is the answer to easing suffering. The selfish part of us tells us to be concerned only with our own happiness – do what is in our best interest first. This is often manifested in our tendency to ignore suffering. When you act in compassion, you dismiss your ego and put someone else on a pedestal. Are you that humble?

One thing that stops us dead in our tracks when we see someone suffering is when we discover that it can remind us of personal suffering or fear. Do not stop here in selfishness. Use this emotion on your path to compassion. Try for a minute to actually notice that people are suffering. Stop trying to sum up everyone's condition in short sentences. Stop imagining what people's stories are. As yourself – "What do I *really* know about people?" Acknowledge your ignorance of others and their condition. Realize that your condition is largely a mystery to others.

I used to turn off the television when the news came on because it was always so negative – I had compassion fatigue and I made the decision to ignore or avoid the suffering of others. Now I have come to understand that watching the news is a spiritual opportunity.

Being compassionate propels you to others. By practicing Live in Self, you will experience an inner awakening that will result in a brand new perception of the world you live in. You will see yourself in others, and others in you. The truth is that you and I are very alike and we feel the same things. Instead of focusing on the differences between you and the others, identify what you have in common. We are human, need food, need shelter, need love, crave happiness and so much more.

> *"If you want others to be happy,*
> *practice compassion. If you want to*
> *be happy, practice compassion."*
>
> — Dalai Lama XIV—

Compassion does not mean giving people what they want or being gentle all the time. You still have a responsibility to apply judgment to the actions you take and maintain the intention of increasing the other person's happiness. In adult relationships, sometimes we detach with love — this is where you remove yourself from the company of someone without ceasing to care about them in your heart. Be compassionate with wisdom. Wisdom in compassion also implies that your own happiness means as much to you as the happiness of others (even those who mistreat you) – no more and no less!

STATEMENT OF INTENTION: As a person who has led a privileged life, it is my responsibility to give something back to others. In order to do this, I will let go of my pride and be humble. I will choose to see myself in others and others in me. I know the tightness of my heart can be dissolved through compassionate acts towards myself and others. I will allow compassion to propel me towards others and I will not forget to be self-compassionate. I will work towards unconditional compassion.

CHAPTER 18: Cultivating Compassion 101

I believe that cultivating compassion has the potential to change your life – it can indeed make you happy. I work on developing it by practicing it daily. Compassion is defined as "sympathetic pity and concern for the suffering and misfortunes of others". It does not mean tolerance or acceptance of abuse. Synonyms for compassion are sympathy, empathy, care, concern, sensitivity, warmth, love, tenderness, mercy, tolerance, kindness, and humanity. The antonyms are indifference and cruelty. The Dalai Lama says "If you want others to be happy, practice compassion. If you want to be happy, practice compassion."

In moments when I find myself being uncompassionate, it is out of selfishness. I am often being self-aware but unmindful of my surroundings lost in the restrictedness of tunnel vision. When I practice compassion, my emotions are consistent. The aim of my compassion is to fulfill my lifelong journey to be happy and to help others be happy.

It is so important to pay attention to what is happening in our lives and to respond in a calm manner to life's ebbs and flows.

— Bhakti Mary —

Each morning as a ritual, before I open my eyes, I begin to think to myself about areas where I can express gratitude and I also set personal intentions for the day.

Start your cultivation of compassion by saying this quote from the Dalai Lama:

Today I am fortunate to have woken up, I am alive, I have a precious human life, I am not going to waste it. I am going to use all my energies to develop myself, to expand my heart out to others, to achieve enlightenment for the benefit of all beings, I am going to have kind thoughts towards others, I am not going to get angry or think badly about others, I am going to benefit others as much as I can.

Throughout the day, I use the following instructions for myself: "Now that you have woken up on the right side of the bed, you can begin to develop internal empathy for others. Quit being centered on self. Remember the old Golden Rule? Stop imposing on others what you would not choose for yourself. Allow yourself to imagine the suffering of others. Recognize what you have in common with other people – that you seek compassion, love, and kindness. Desire for people to be free of suffering. Do something kind that will help ease the suffering of others."

When I generalize and say "others", it is on purpose. Cultivating compassion towards friends AND enemies alike is very important.

CHAPTER 19: Finding a Specific Purpose

The fear of failure often propels people in a direction incongruent to their dreams. The lack of knowing what one's dream is can also cause one to wander aimlessly. One thing is for sure – if we are afraid of failure and do not pursue our dreams fully, they will be impossible to achieve. In the journey to our dreams, there will be mountains to descend from and valleys to climb out of. One step at a time, we will make it;

To simply wake up every morning a better person than when I went to bed.

— Sidney Poitier —

But what if one feels their purpose is a mystery? In my case, I still do not know what my dream or purpose is. As I move closer to discovering what it is, my aim is to continuously learn and strive to become better than who I am. I believe that the world will be better when I am better. I began Live in Self because of some advice that my father gave me regarding the fear of failure.

He said, "if you think you want to do something, just try it. Try anything. If you fail at one thing, try another thing." I have always enjoyed discussing how to become a better person with friends and family. This discussion is now expanded to include you.

As I explore this life work, I learn with you about becoming a better person. What endeavors are teaching you to be a better person? Is the core of everyone's dream really becoming a better person — given what I know, I think this might be the case, but I recognize that becoming a better person is subjective or customized depending on our personal perspectives and outlooks. If you feel you lack purpose, join me in taking the journey to becoming a better person.

CHAPTER 20: The Daffodil Principle

I saved this article called *The Daffodil Garden* by Jaroldeen Asplund Edwards many years ago because I thought it would be worth revisiting and sharing with others at a later date. You will enjoy this reading...

....

Several times my daughter had telephoned to say, "Mother, you must come see the daffodils before they are over." I wanted to go, but it was a two-hour drive from Laguna to Lake Arrowhead.

"I will come next Tuesday," I promised, a little reluctantly, on her third call.

Next Tuesday dawned cold and rainy. Still, I had promised, and so I drove there. When I finally walked into Carolyn's house and hugged and greeted my grandchildren, I said, "Forget the daffodils, Carolyn! The road is invisible in the clouds and fog, and there is nothing in the world except you and these children that I want to see bad enough to drive another inch!"

My daughter smiled calmly and said, "We drive in this all the time, Mother."

"Well, you won't get me back on the road until it clears, and then

I'm heading for home!" I assured her.

"I was hoping you'd take me over to the garage to pick up my car."

"How far will we have to drive?"

"Just a few blocks," Carolyn said. "I'll drive. I'm used to this."

After several minutes, I had to ask, "Where are we going? This isn't the way to the garage!"

"We're going to my garage the long way," Carolyn smiled, "by way of the daffodils."

"Carolyn," I said sternly, "please turn around."

"It's all right, Mother, I promise. You will never forgive yourself if you miss this experience."

After about twenty minutes, we turned onto a small gravel road and I saw a small church. On the far side of the church, I saw a hand-lettered sign that said, "Daffodil Garden."

We got out of the car and each took a child's hand, and I followed Carolyn down the path. Then, we turned a corner of the path, and I looked up and gasped. Before me lay the most glorious sight. It looked as though someone had taken a great vat of gold and poured it down over the mountain peak and slopes. The flowers were planted in majestic, swirling patterns- great ribbons and swaths of deep orange, white, lemon yellow, salmon pink, saffron, and butter yellow. Each different-colored variety was planted as a group so that it swirled and flowed like its own river with its own unique hue. There were five acres of flowers.

"But who has done this?" I asked Carolyn.

"It's just one woman," Carolyn answered. "She lives on the property. That's her home."

Carolyn pointed to a well-kept A-frame house that looked small and modest in the midst of all that glory. We walked up to the house. On the patio, we saw a poster. "Answers to the Questions I Know You Are Asking" was the headline.

The first answer was a simple one. "50,000 bulbs," it read. The second answer was, "One at a time, by one woman. Two hands, two feet, and very little brain." The third answer was, "Began in 1958."

There it was, The Daffodil Principle.

For me, that moment was a life-changing experience. I thought of this woman whom I had never met, who, more than forty years before, had begun ~ one bulb at a time ~ to bring her vision of beauty and joy to an obscure mountain top. Still, just planting one bulb at a time, year after year, had changed the world. This unknown woman had forever changed the world in which she lived. She had created something of ineffable (indescribable) magnificence, beauty, and inspiration.

The principle her daffodil garden taught is one of the greatest principles of celebration. That is, learning to move toward our goals and desires one step at a time ~ often just one baby- step at a time ~ and learning to love the doing, learning to use the accumulation of time. When we multiply tiny pieces of time with small increments of daily effort, we too will find we can accomplish magnificent things. We can change the world.

"It makes me sad in a way," I admitted to Carolyn. "What might I have accomplished if I had thought of a wonderful goal thirty- five or forty years ago and had worked away at it 'one bulb at a time' through all those years. Just think what I might have been able to achieve!"

My daughter summed up the message of the day in her usual direct way. "Start tomorrow," she said.

It's so pointless to think of the lost hours of yesterdays. The way to make learning a lesson of celebration instead of a cause for regret is to only ask, "How can I put this to use today?"

We convince ourselves that life will be better after we get married, have a baby, then another. Then we are frustrated that the kids aren't old enough and we'll be more content when they are. After that, we're frustrated that we have teenagers to deal with. We will certainly be happy when they are out of that stage.

We tell ourselves that our life will be complete when our spouse gets his or her act together, when we get a nicer car, when we are able to go on a nice vacation, or when we retire. The truth is there's no better time to be happy than right now. If not now, when? Your life will always be filled with challenges. It's best to admit this to yourself and decide to be happy anyway.

Happiness is the way. So, treasure every moment that you have and treasure it more because you shared it with someone special;

special to spend your time with and remember that time waits for no one.

So, stop waiting until your car or home is paid off. Until you get a new car or home. Until your kids leave the house. Until you go back to school. Until you finish school. Until you lose 10 lbs. Until you gain 10 lbs. Until you get married. Until you get a divorce. Until you have kids. Until you retire. Until summer. Until spring. Until winter. Until fall. Until you die. There is no better time than right now to be happy.

Happiness is a journey, not a destination. So work like you do not need money. Love like you've never been hurt. And dance like no one's watching.

The daffodil garden mentioned in this story really does exist and anyone can visit during peak bloom time, early March to early April. The garden is located below Running Springs, California, in the San Bernardino Mountains. From the city of Highland (about 60 miles east of downtown Los Angeles), take Highway 330 toward Running Springs. Drive

14 miles into the mountains to the intersection of Live Oak Dr. and Fredalba. Turn right on Fredalba and proceed one mile. Park in the church parking lot. From there, signs will direct you.

Stop waiting to be happy. Decide today to view life as a lesson and decide to be happy; take each step necessary to be happy right where you are.

— Bhakti Mary —

CHAPTER 21: Turning Life Into A Living Meditation

You can turn your life into a living meditation if you stop looking back, stop leaning forward, and start living in the present moment.

Stop holding on to your old normal and accept the new normal. When you hold onto your history, you do so at the expense of your destiny. When you resist the reality of what is, you suffer. Transcend the past. Hate your past? Do your inner work! Stop leaning back – this causes depression. Realize that no experience is wasted whether good or bad. Everything that has happened to us has value and contains a lesson. Do not waste a hurt – use it for good!

Do not lean forward – this causes anxiety and worry which substantially curtails the joy and fullness of life. Eckhart Tolle says that worry pretends to be necessary but serves no useful purpose. You cannot predict or control the future! Also, stop looking at 'potential' – it is not real – it is a fantasy.

Stop and slow down! Be present. Accept the present. The key to unlocking self is acceptance.

See the present where the joy resides. Turn up the volume on life! Pray for birth of clarity in your aims and call moments of clarity into being.

How do you feel? Start by simply being aware of your breath – move to your thoughts – thoughts create reality. How do you talk to yourself? How you think changes how you feel which changes how you behave. You can change your thoughts! If you do not like your thoughts, stop resisting and start changing them. What you resist will just persist. Be transformed by the renewal of your mind. Live in self! Make life a living meditation.

Be FULLY available for all experiences. Stop resisting the challenges in front of you; welcome them and you will open the door for opportunity and growth.

Seize the opportunities! If you are facing a challenge, know that this too shall pass and you are not the trial. Challenges are simply a call to move you into something greater. Feel what is happening and know that it is leading you to something greater.

CHAPTER 22: Reacting Positively to Stress

Stress is a natural and inevitable part of our lives. It cannot be eliminated but you can change your approach and reaction to stress. Your body can react to stress in the same manner it reacts to joy and courage. Let us get better at handling stress.

When I was deployed to Iraq in 2009, my mom stayed in my home and took care of my son part time. She told a story of how she took him to take photos with Santa and he was all over the place; she was trying to get him to behave and so he started hitting her...she eventually took him home and told him that he was being bad and he told her not to hurt him. She then explained to him that he hurt her by hitting her on her head and so he kissed her on the head and said he was sorry and told her it was all better.

Then she sent him to his room and eventually he came out and she told him that he would have to play alone for a while. So he went to the living room and he began to assemble a hard puzzle. He put the whole thing together until the last two pieces. Then he took the last two pieces to my mom in her room. He said, "Please help grandma." She went out to the living room and discovered that he had put together the whole puzzle except for two pieces. He had saved one for her and one for him so they could finish it together. This was an extremely stressful situation for both of them, and they both used different techniques to overcome it.

Learning relaxation techniques to employ when presented with stress can calm you down and improve your mood. View your stress response as helpful – rise to challenges. How you think and how you act change how you view stress. Connecting with others under stress (caring) creates resilience. Use your compassionate heart to find joy in connecting with others...trust yourself to handle life's challenges.

You may wonder how to practice relaxation techniques in front of others. The times when I am most stressed tend to be in conversation with others or when I feel emotionally invested in someone or something. During these times, I silently begin to relax my face and body one part at a time; I silently slow my breath and take deep relaxing breaths. I choose silence over speech until I can compose myself and handle the challenge I am faced with. By this time, I have calmed down and chosen a wise and positive response that shows that I care. Now I have a fidget spinner; maybe I will incorporate that in my responses.

In opportunities to connect with others, how can we show that we care more? How can we respond to stressful situations by continuing to connect and care?

CHAPTER 23: Inspiring Others – Maya Angelou

Maya Angelou's powerful and wise words will never lose their relevance. She will be admired by all generations and if we read and heed some of her advice, we can live our lives better. In her memory, here are some of my favorite Maya Angelou quotes. I hope they will inspire you as much as they inspire me to treat others well, forgive everybody, thrive at living, be positive, be courageous, keep loving, never give up, and to be my bright and bold self.

TREAT OTHERS WELL.

• Try to be a rainbow in someone's cloud.

• I've learned that people will forget what you said, people will forget what you did, but people will never forget how you made them feel.

• I've learned that you shouldn't go through life with a catcher's mitt on both hands; you need to be able to throw something back.

• It's one of the greatest gifts you can give yourself, to forgive.

FORGIVE EVERYBODY.

• I've learned that even when I have pains, I do not have to be one.

• We can learn to see each other and see ourselves in each other and recognize that human beings are more alike than we are unalike.

• It is time for parents to teach young people early on that in diversity there is beauty and there is strength. We all should know that diversity makes for a rich tapestry, and we must understand that all the threads of that tapestry are equal in value no matter their color.

THRIVE AT LIVING.

• What is a fear of living? It's being preeminently afraid of dying. It is not doing what you came here to do, out of timidity and spinelessness. The antidote is to take full responsibility for yourself — for the time you take up and the space you occupy. If you do not know what you're here to do, then just do some good.

• My mission in life is not merely to survive, but to thrive; and to do so with some passion, some compassion, some humor, and some style.

BE POSITIVE.

• You are the sum total of everything you've ever seen, heard, eaten, smelled, been told, forgot — it's all there. Everything influences each of us, and because of that I try to make sure that my experiences are positive.

• Whining is not only graceless, but it can be dangerous. It can alert a brute that a victim is in the neighborhood.

BE COURAGEOUS.

• One isn't necessarily born with courage, but one is born with potential. Without courage, we cannot practice any other virtue with consistency. We cannot be kind, true, merciful, generous, or honest.

• History, despite its wrenching pain, cannot be unlived, but if faced with courage, need not be lived again.

KEEP LOVING.

• Have enough courage to trust love one more time. And always one more time.

• Love recognizes no barriers. It jumps hurdles, leaps fences, penetrates walls to arrive at its destination full of hope.

NEVER GIVE UP.

• We may encounter many defeats but we must not be defeated.

• You may not control all the events that happen to you, but you can decide not to be reduced by them.

• If you do not like something, change it. If you cannot change it, change your attitude.

BE YOUR BRIGHT AND BOLD SELF.

• Nothing can dim the light which shines from within.

• If you're always trying to be normal, you will never know how amazing you can be.

• You alone are enough. You have nothing to prove to anybody.

CHAPTER 24: The Stranger is You

I heard an audio blurb that intrigued me on BBC News. It was the story of a man named Johnny Benjamin, a diagnosed schizoaffective man (at age 20), who had nearly taken his life through suicide. Schizoaffective disorder is a combination of schizophrenia and bipolar. Johnny began hearing voices in his head at the age of 10 and believed that he was being watched by cameras everywhere he went. This continued through his teen years and he began to have a repeating mantra – "Perhaps it would be better off if I wasn't here."

Johnny had been saved from jumping off the bridge by a stranger's words. The stranger said he also was schizophrenic – he said "I've been through this" and told Johnny "a few years later I'm on top of the world" – "it will get better". No one had ever told Johnny that he could get better and he had always been led to believe that things would get worse. Johnny was in a hospital where he was surrounded by people just like him who he felt were not getting better. He had put himself in that category of people − the ones who weren't getting better fast enough and may never get better.

The stranger gave Johnny a sense of hope − his outlook was changed. Even when people around us aren't getting better, we can get better!

Johnny credits cognitive therapy with helping him break the patterns of negative thoughts. He also credits the love and support of people during that difficult time. Medication also helped with his recovery; Johnny is completely medication free now!

Johnny says that people often speak about illness when it regards bodily organs but not the brain, not the mind − because we think this will alter how people think about us, it will turn us into a burden, it will confirm that we have indeed let our family and friends down. As far as my interactions with people with mental illness, I struggle to understand what they are going through and why they cannot just "will" themselves better. I tend to think that the human will is strong enough to change negative thoughts to positive thoughts...but, as I watched Johnny Benjamin, I came to some better realizations that I want to share.

As you go through the day, remember that the stranger is you.

It is imperative to show compassion – to speak kindly. You do not need to necessarily understand what people are going through, and, as hard as we try, we can never truly put ourselves in someone else's shoes. We lack the full story on everyone we encounter but we are constantly presented with opportunities to act with compassion. We can and should speak of hope for others. We should not look at struggles as being the path to helplessness. Your words matter to people – people you do not necessarily know. THE STRANGER IS YOU!

If you know anyone with mental illness, want to know more about mental illness, or you have mental illness, watching Johnny Benjamin's videos WILL change you.

CHAPTER 25: Reflecting on Shooting Stars

One Friday night, I set my alarm to rise at 2 a.m. to check out the Camelopardalid meteor shower. A CNN article describing the event was titled "Heads-Up! Stargazers on alert for rare, possibly epic meteor shower". In Ohio, the skies are not always clear enough, but on this night, they were clear horizon to horizon. My then boyfriend had said he would watch with me; after all, he was the one who alerted me of the event. After trying to wake my boyfriend three times, I decided to make some hot tea and head out alone to my back yard.

"I would rather be ashes than dust!

I would rather that my spark should burn out in a brilliant blaze than it should be stifled by dry-rot.

I would rather be a superb meteor, every atom of me in magnificent glow, than a sleepy and permanent planet. The function of man is to live, not to exist.

CHERRY

*I shall not waste my days trying to
prolong them. I shall use my time."*

— Jack London —

A meteor shower is a celestial event in which a number of meteors are observed to radiate from a point in the night sky. The meteor shower that I usually try to observe is the Perseids meteor shower which peaks around 12 August each year; during the Perseids meteor shower, over one meteor per minute might be visible. In basic terms, one can see a lot of shooting stars or meteors. As I laid outside staring at the sky, I thought that this event mirrored life in many regards.

Life's experiences are not always as exciting as predicted. Sometimes we learn about and anticipate an exciting event. We wait for it to happen and then the experience is not as exciting as we hoped. I stared at the sky for about 1.5 hours and I saw 4 shooting stars and 2 satellites. Between each one, I wondered when the next one would come along. I couldn't predict it...I simply had to wait with no guarantees. After the fourth one, I decided to retire for the night. I wondered what happened to the "EPIC" meteor shower?

Life's excitement is often short lived. A shooting star is often over in under a second. Appreciate the good times no matter how short in duration they may be. You do not know when the next one is coming!

If you are not awake and focused, you may miss out on the present. If you're not looking, sometimes you will miss the shooting stars. To see a shooting star, you have to be looking at the sky at the spot where the shooting star is, otherwise you will miss it. In life you have to focus on something. You have to stop and focus. Live in the now!

If you want to experience life, sometimes you have to be willing to be alone. Sometimes, we hope to share something amazing with someone and we find ourselves alone. That is not a reason to abandon the experience. Loneliness is not just cause to abandon the experience of the here and now! Be still and enjoy the present moment.

CHAPTER 26: You Are Never Invisible

I found myself at the auto dealer very early one morning to get unscheduled car maintenance. When you arrive anywhere early in the morning, you encounter people who are either so wide awake that it irritates you or delights you or people are in such a mobile slumber that you can barely get their attention.

In the dealership, I went to grab a cup of coffee which seemed like the logical thing to do on a cold 40-degree morning in May in Ohio. There was an older gentleman who definitely agreed — as you can imagine he was the wide awake kind. It did not irritate me...it was a breath of fresh air. His friendly demeanor followed me into the dealership waiting area where he cheerfully commented on my healthy choice for a morning snack — baby carrots.

Shortly after I took my seat, another older gentleman entered the room with a portable oxygen tank in tow. As he sat down, he struggled to breathe. It served as a close reminder to me on how life is always hanging on just by a thread. This man wasn't really interested in talking to anyone and seemed more interested in and focused on breathing.

Other people continued to pile into the waiting area. Most did not want to talk. One lady was intent on getting her work started on her laptop. Others were just content watching the HLN Morning Express with Robin Meade; I had turned the TV to that show since I was the first one to sit in the waiting area that morning.

Watching the news in a large group of people is always interesting. There can be awkward moments of silence. This particular morning, the moment of silence came when Robin Meade discussed New Hampshire Police Commissioner Robert Copeland, an 82-year-old man who won his public office after running unopposed for re-election in a town of 6300 residents (20 black residents). Mr. Copeland was the subject of public discussion after he refused to apologize for calling then President Barack Obama the N-word.

After the story was briefly discussed, one could have heard a pin drop in the waiting area. I was the only minority in the room and felt very alone. No one said a word.

Is silence consent or support? Does it matter? Throughout the next half hour, I had to spend in the waiting area, I had a lump in my throat and a knot in my stomach paired with a feeling of loneliness.

I wondered what people really thought of me, of my skin color, of my gender, my clothes, etc. Then, I decided that if I was going to spend all morning at the dealership, I needed to just be myself. I didn't know what these people thought about me, and they weren't going to tell me, so why was I worrying about it?

I needed to let people's decisions, opinions, and thoughts sit with them. Later, I took the opportunity to laugh out loud to clear the air in the room when the news story aired of an elephant who was taking a dip in the Gulf because someone wanted him to be present at their birthday party. I engaged the wide-a w a k e gentleman in a discussion of how wonderful or weird this experience must have been for the elephant and the oxygen tank gentleman joined in.

I could not change my skin color or my gender but I could be my best self. BE YOUR BEST SELF. Let others decide for themselves, and then let their decision lie with them. I sat in the waiting area for another hour and as new people filed in, I smiled at them.

While we should remain mindful of other's opinions, we must be careful how we let it impact us.

Do not shrink – even if you think you
can disappear inside yourself,
everyone will still see you!

YOU ARE NOT INVISIBLE.

— Bhakti Mary —

If you are truly living inside out, you might feel alone at times. Be comfortable in your own skin. JUST BE!

CHAPTER 27: Being the Water

In military circles, I often hear the phrase "Flexibility is the key to airpower". I think flexibility is the key to life — flexibility in emotional, mental and spiritual capacities.

Imagine a large tree. The roots are our belief system — the tree should be solid but not so solid that it becomes completely uprooted at the onset or occurrence of a major storm. The optimal tree is the one continues to grow, is flexible, and is rooted. Be a redwood!

Sometimes our workplace drives us to be rigid and routine — to operate inside the box or to color inside the lines. Working for the military and in the federal government has certainly brought its excessive share of "in the box" experiences. In our personal life, we have an opportunity to operate outside the box or to define new borders. What does this mean? Operating outside the box is being flexible and open-minded. It is being willing to challenge self from time to time. It is moving with the flow at times. It is being open to people and their suggestions, ideas, concepts, experiences and outlook.

Flexibility is a life enhancer. Cognitive flexibility is present when we are adaptive to our surroundings and when we can move past habitual responses. The ability to overcome previously held habits or beliefs signifies that we have an awareness of alternate options in any given situation. Being flexible can certainly help us cope with stressful, unique or uncomfortable situations.

Choose today and every day to be flexible. Remember endings are also beginnings. I realize now that this is truly the key to success in relationships. Choosing battles is about flexibility and then knowing where to start and end relationships is also critical.

Be the water in people's lives...the nourishment. Approach situations with an unbiased attitude; have a fair mindset to guide your responses. Do not get caught up in being right or wrong. Listen to someone express an opinion and refrain from imposing your position. Dismiss your prideful self. Recognize that ultimately, everyone is connected along the same wavelength.

David Jones says it perfectly - "Planning is helpful. If you do not know what you want, you'll seldom get it. But, no matter how well you plan, you will fare better if you expect the unexpected. The unexpected, by nature, comes unseen, and unthought, unenvisioned. All you can do is plan to go unplanned, prepare to be unprepared, make going with the flow part of your agenda, for the most successful among us envision, plan, and prepare, but cast all aside as needed, while those who are unable to go with the flow often suffer, if they survive."

CHAPTER 28: Finding Your Safe Haven

It is very important to have a personal safe haven to go to occassionally. A personal safe haven is a place of refuge and comfort where you can go to reflect, to be renewed, to find peace, to let down your guard, to be calm, to find solitude. This can be a physical or mental place. Your safe haven can be anything you need it to be.

As you are considering what your safe haven might be, perform self-discovery with regard to what feeds your soul and what speaks to you.

Some examples of personal safe havens are:

- looking at a picture of an enjoyable place

- touching an object that promotes positive thoughts

- listening to a song

- meditating

- exercising

When you feel like the world is coming crashing in around you or when you just feel out of balance, retreat to your safe haven for 5-10 minutes. Refocus, reprioritize, and find your center. Then *return to life*.

If you go into any home décor store, you can usually find décor with the phrase Keep Calm and Carry On. *Keep Calm and Carry On* was the phrase on a motivational poster produced by the British government in 1939 after the start of WWII for the purpose of raising the morale of the British public in the aftermath of predicted mass air attacks on major cities. While the poster was never put on public display, it is now is a popular phrase displayed in many homes.

Sometimes I go to my personal safe haven to keep calm and carry on because while we cannot always choose what happens to us, we can work to improve our response.

CHAPTER 29: The Beauty of Desiderata

One of my favorite pieces of prose was written by Max Ehrmann in 1927. It is titled *Desiderata*. I do not think it needs any commentary because it speaks for itself. Here is the text (parts that speak to me are bolded):

Go placidly amid the noise and haste, and **remember what peace there may be in silence.**

As far as possible without surrender **be on good terms with all persons.**

Speak your truth quietly and clearly; and **listen to others**, even the dull and ignorant; they too have their story. Avoid loud and aggressive persons, they are vexations to the spirit.

If you compare yourself with others, you may become vain and bitter; for always there will be greater and lesser persons than yourself.

Enjoy your achievements as well as your plans. Keep interested in your career, however humble; it is a real possession in the changing fortunes of time. Exercise caution in your business affairs; for the world is full of trickery. But let this not blind you to what virtue there is; many persons strive for high ideals; and **everywhere life is full of heroism**.

Be yourself. Especially, do not feign affection. Neither be critical about love; for in the face of all aridity and disenchantment it is as perennial as the grass.

Take kindly the counsel of the years, gracefully surrendering the things of youth.

Nurture strength of spirit to shield you in sudden misfortune. But **do not distress yourself with imaginings**. Many fears are born of fatigue and loneliness. Beyond a wholesome discipline, **be gentle with yourself**.

You are a child of the universe, no less than the trees and the stars; you have a right to be here. And whether or not it is clear to you, no doubt the universe is unfolding as it should.

Therefore **be at peace with God, whatever you conceive Him to be**, and whatever your labors and aspirations, in the noisy confusion of life **keep peace with your soul**. With all its sham, drudgery and broken dreams, it is still a beautiful world. Be cheerful. **Strive to be happy**.

CHAPTER 30: Finding Simple Ways to Live in the Present

I was on a plane once during the evening and had the opportunity to see a beautiful sunset on takeoff. My first instinct when I see something I like or something that is beautiful is to grab my phone and take a picture. What are my children going to do with a picture of a sunset? I am not sure there is a use for it, but nonetheless I look at a lot of life through the phone screen. I have over 20,000 cell phone photos on my computer. As I write this, I can hear some of you gasping.

When I saw the sunset, I tried taking a few pictures with my phone, but I could not get any that looked like what I was actually seeing. Then I had an ah-ha moment.

I have recently been trying to learn ways to live in the present, and this was the perfect opportunity. Technology was causing me to miss the moment. The sunset was most beautiful through my own eyes and if I continued looking at it through my phone screen, I would miss it altogether.

I put my phone down and chose to be fully present in that moment. I chose to live! I savored the sunset.

What opportunities have you had lately to live in the present?

CHAPTER 31: Relaxing In The Present Moment

I once read an article where yoga was being promoted as a "form of physical fitness" and meditation as a "form of mental fitness". I believe meditation can serve as a form of physical and mental fitness. Many people embrace yoga and meditation but they are not interested in the religious context of it. Mark Nunberg, co- founder of Common Ground Meditation Center in Minneapolis, says meditation is "training the mind to be in the present moment in a relaxed way". Do not you want to be able to lower your stress and increase your ability to focus – this just scratches the surface of the beneficial physical and mental effects of meditation on the brain. Neuroscientists are monitoring brain activity during meditation and confirming what serious meditators have known all along – the brain can be trained just like a muscle.

Most of you probably spend a significant amount of your day at work. Is it possible to **relax in the**

present at work? I think so. Here are some of my ideas on how to do so.

INNER MOUTH

Pick a positive word – peace, joy, happiness, love, beautiful, calm, serenity. Sit still, close your eyes and calm your breathing.

Say the word in your mind for a minute and bring your mind back to the word when it wanders. Repeat as often as you can.

INNER EAR

Put a peaceful song in your cell phone to listen to. Take 5 minutes to think about each noise you hear in the song. Check out.

CONSCIOUS NOSE

Sit at your desk. Continue the work you are doing but focus on your breathing. Slow your breathing and take long slow breaths. This can be used as a de-stressing technique during any period of extreme stress.

EXTEND YOUR POSITIVITY

Make a day more positive by thinking of a wish of success when you see your coworkers. Be sincere. Train your mind to think about the positive aspect of people; it will change how you interact.

By doing these simple things, you can be joyful and relaxed in the present moment. Work can become enjoyable despite its mundane and monotonous nature. Do you have other ideas for relaxing during your daily routine?

CHAPTER 32: The Importance of Hope

It was the Christmas season in 2015. I was part of a Facebook group called *No Excuse Moms*. In this group, women cheer each other on when they are struggling, surviving or thriving. It is so important to possess the capability to lift people up no matter where they are in their life and I am working to become better at this.

I happened to read a comment to a main post that spoke to me. I immediately felt compelled to act. A mother was expressing her worry about not being able to get her children anything for Christmas so I asked her to please contact me because I wanted to help.

My offer brought this mother to tears and through Facebook messenger, the woman described some items that her children - a 13-year-old boy and 8-year-old boy - might be interested in. Now if they are anything like my 9-year-old boy, they must get the items they want otherwise the world will end. As a mother, I can relate to the desire to please my child and to see the smile that comes when you give a child a gift. The thought of not being able to do this scared the mother. My offer gave her the courage to ask her boys what they wanted because now she had hope and faith that they may actually receive the items.

What was she feeling? Hopelessness. She told me a story of a gentleman that comes to the restaurant she works at. Every time, before he leaves, he picks a table and pays for the meal. When she asked why he did this, he said simply to give people hope.

I immediately went to Amazon and placed an order for a skateboard, football, two video games, an Uno game, a soccer ball, and a nice bracelet for mom. Two days later, the items had already started to arrive.

When you are able to give hope, grab the opportunity. My generosity allowed the mother to feel blessed and allowed her to rest at night. She relayed to me that she now had a "renewed spirit" and "peace of mind". My act of kindness gave her "the strength to push on".

I appreciated greatly that this mother had the courage to answer my offer to help and that she allowed me to be generous in creating a moment of joy for her family. She said to me "I believe God sent you to me right when I needed a blessing so much. I appreciate you." I still reach out to her to offer my support virtually because the truth is sometimes our toughest journeys are also our longest journeys and the support of a stranger can make all the difference.

Technology can help us to perform great acts. You may complain about social media, but it allowed me to reach a stranger in Florida and offer help. You may complain about Amazon but it allowed me to rapidly deploy gifts to a family in need during a holiday season.

My intention was simply to transfer the spirit of hope, generosity, and renewal to a mother in need. Answer the call to help, and use all tools in your possession to achieve these simple acts of compassion that can change the trajectory of the human spirit for we are all connected near and afar.

CHAPTER 33: Do Not Delay Your Resolutions

You do not have to wait until January 1st to make resolutions. Any time of the year is a great time to make goals. Let us get started!

1) THINK AT THE MOUNTAIN TOP: Begin by finding a quiet place to sit and reflect with pen and paper in hand. Think about changes you would like to make in your life. Take notes in the areas of physical, mental, spiritual, financial, and social fitness. Start with large "10,000 foot" goals.

2) GET TO GROUND LEVEL: Break down the "10,000 foot" goals into smaller actions. Focus your actions on forming and establishing habits and behaviors that will serve you for a lifetime. Choose your goals and actions wisely – make sure they are things you can stick with and factor in variety and breaks. Ensure each goal has a time-activated plan associated with it.

3) LET OTHERS KNOW: Discuss your list with your loved ones. This can be a child, a friend, a spouse, a parent or a co-worker. Let them know you

would appreciate their encouragement along the way. When they encourage you, channel the positive energy that accompanies the encouragement towards achieving your goals.

4) ACCOUNTABILITY: Select a trustworthy reliable friend(s) and ask them if they will be your accountability partner and mentor. This will help you stay focused on your goal.

5) VISIBILITY: Print a small copy of your list and keep it in your wallet or purse. Email a copy to yourself and post a copy in a visible place in the house that you visit often such as the kitchen or bathroom. Write your action steps in your daily planner, calendar, or schedule.

6) START NOW: Start following the plan immediately. Focus on the process and take each step one at a time.

7) NO BLAME ALLOWED: Look beyond "I cannot". Focus on "I can" and "I am". Do not allow yourself to blame other people or circumstances for not carrying out your steps. Identify your self-

defeating behaviors and deal with them instead of continuing to do them.

8) REWARD YOURSELF: Pencil in rewards in your planner for when you complete steps or accomplish goals.

9) RECOMMIT: From time to time, you might fall off track with your resolution. We all do. Use the next Monday as the day to recommit to your goals. Allow yourself a weekly chance to get back on track with your goals.

CHAPTER 34: Recommitting to Your Goals

The first week of a month is a perfect time to reassess, reset, or recommit yourself to your goals. Always allow yourself a chance to get back on track!

REASSESS: If have have already set goals, reassessing them is something you should do from time to time. See if the original goals you set are being met, if they need to be, or if they are no longer relevant. If the goal is still relevant, make sure you are still on a path that allows you to reach your personal best.

RESET: Did you fall off the bandwagon? Have you lost motivation? It's never too late to get back on track! If you still want to accomplish your goals, make a plan to get started again. Remember that accountability and visibility are key to resetting. Let others know that you are getting on track and you would appreciate their encouragement along the way. Select one or two close friends and ask them if they will be your accountability partner and mentor. Finally, keep a visual reminder of your goals in your wallet/purse/planner and post one in a visible place in your house.

RECOMMIT: Remember, no blame is allowed. Focus on "I can" and "I am". Other people are not responsible for your lack of past commitments. Continue to work on yourself! Keep identifying your self-defeating behaviors and deal with them instead of continuing to do them.

CHAPTER 35: Top 9 New Year's Resolutions

Everyone thinks about what they will do better when the New Year rolls around. Here are 9 ideas to get you started!

1. **Quit an Addiction.** Whether it's excessive social media, smoking, soda drinking, bad spending habits, excessive drinking or another habit, acknowledge that it is doing you no good. Find a way and resolve to quit it.

2. **Learn Something New.** Add value to your experiences and interactions by continuously learning. There are no excuses on this goal— the information age ensures an infinite number of learning opportunities are available to you.

3. **Get Fit.** Start eating healthy and make time for fitness. If you do not take care of yourself to the best of your ability, do not expect or ask anyone to take care of you!

4. **Lose the Loans.** Pay off a specific amount of debt each month. Financial obligations are a

primary source of stress for most people so take steps to lighten your load!

5. **Sack the Stress.** Find a safe haven for relaxing. Pamper yourself from time to time. Stop worrying about what other people think of you. Most of all, get to bed early for a feeling of rejuvenation.

6. **Volunteer.** Give back and make the world a better place to live in through contributing your actions. Do something positive for people in need.

7. **Organize It.** Declutter your home, work desk, car, garage or any other needy area. Begin with one small spot in order to build up confidence. Then stand back and notice how even a small effort to declutter helps you to live a more organized and positive life. Do something to track your daily activities so you can stop being forgetful and procrastinating. Being more deliberate can facilitate going through the day with ease by being more organized.

8. **Be Angelic.** This applies to women and men. Take on a positive approach to life and start seeing your glass as half full, not half empty. Quit judging others and vow not to worry about people judging you. Find the positive – it surrounds you already!

9. **Make Time for Family and Friends.** A work-life balance is key to a stress-free life. Make it a priority to spend time with family and friends no matter what! Schedule them into your calendar just like you would an important work meeting. Relationships often give you the greatest amount of fulfillment. Do not let them fall to the wayside.

CHAPTER 36: Forming Simplistic Routines

Simple routines are key to making the best use of your time while at the same time developing yourself as a whole person. Many people have excuses for why they do not take care of themselves when the truth is that they have created absurd routines for each self-care action that give them ample reason for ignoring themselves. There is no excuse.

God did not make most of us special by requiring that we go through complicated routines to take care of ourselves. We tend to want to establish ourselves as being different from everyone else because we have some unique excuse as to why we cannot take care of ourselves or we cling to some historically unique excuse to justify how we got stuck where we are.

When we can let go of these things, then we can begin to clearly see how simple life can be. We can begin minimizing cost in terms of time and money and begin maximizing whole person development.

When you eat healthy food, you feel better.

When you look nice, you feel confident.

When you have faith, you feel hopeful.

Health Tip #1:

Make healthy meals simple - breakfast prep should take 15 minutes or less most days. Breakfast is the most important meal of the day, but the morning tends to be the busiest time of the day. You're waking up - maybe you are not a morning person, you are rushing to get kids on the bus, or you are rushing to get to work on time. To stay on track for a healthy lifestyle, you must have something quick and easy.

Self-care often involves putting ourselves first - AND - putting ourselves first does not mean we are putting others last. We are choosing to start our day with a simple routine that is best for us like a healthy breakfast. When I make sure I get a healthy breakfast in the morning, no one was put last, but I did take care of myself first thing in the day.

I am 31 weeks pregnant and soon a new baby girl will be here. I will be spending a lot of time breastfeeding so I want to have simple breakfast recipes that are healthy and easy for my fiancé to prepare for the family. He will be tired too so something simple is key! Going in, we won't have an excuse for not eating a healthy breakfast.

People tend to either have a financial excuse or 'lack of time' excuse for why they aren't eating healthy. I smile whenever someone quotes one of these factors as the reason they cannot eat healthy because I know that neither constitutes a valid reason.

Today for breakfast I had a parfait. This took less than 5 minutes to make and since I have increased my caloric intake due to pregnancy, I made a double serving.

Beauty Tip #1:

Create beauty routines that are simple and require little time. Anyone who knows me, knows I love looking nice and I try to look nice most of the time. I have even started realizing the importance of looking nice at home when I do not leave the house. I developed a beauty routine that takes between 10 and 30 minutes. Where I could save more time is in choosing an outfit to wear...this takes me way too long!

When I make sure I look nice in the morning, I teach my children the importance of looking nice and I set a good example for them. Looking put together will help them as they grow up, as they seek jobs, and when they find themselves in a position where their confidence is waning. It's a good habit to have.

People tend to either have a financial excuse or a 'lack of time' excuse for why they do not look nice. I smile whenever someone quotes one of these factors as the reason they cannot look put together because I know that neither constitutes a valid reason.

I straighten my hair sometimes. When I do, I receive a lot of compliments and people always ask how long it took me because they assume that this takes a long time. I have very long hair - almost flowing down my entire back now. The truth is it only takes me a total of 30-45 minutes extra to straighten it. Here's how I do it:

1) Shampoo and condition hair as part of normal shower routine.

2) Comb as part of normal post shower routine.

3) Add pea sized drop of L'oreal Smooth Intense Straight Perfecting Balm.

4) Tie hair in a bun and leave to dry for about 24 hours. (saves blow drying time and hair damage)

5) Untie and straighten w/ Chi Flat Iron.

Now straightening my hair actually reduces my hair preparation time and saves me money for the next week or two. I don't wash my hair for at least a week, (saves water and time), I don't have to add many hair products to make it look nice (saves money), and I don't spend as much time making it look nice each morning (saves time).

Another thing I consider prior to straightening my hair is the weather for the week. If there's a lot of rain in the forecast, then I choose a more practical style for that week like a simple bun or naturally curly hair.

Spiritual Tip #1:

Incorporate worship or prayer into your normal daily activities. Gratitude is central to my spiritual practice. It keeps me grounded, centered and humble.

People tend to have a lack of time' excuse for why they do not have a spiritual practice. I smile whenever someone quotes this factor as the reason they do not have a spiritual routine because I know that it cannot and should not constitute a valid reason.

As I am typing this blog on Sunday morning, I am playing gospel music which has a spiritual message and serves to make my work a living worship. As I was waking up this morning, I said my prayers of gratitude before I got out of bed.

Spiritual acts don't necessarily have to involve going to church each week or reading a religious text for 15 minutes a day.

Just do what works for you - whatever makes you whole - with the time and money you have. And if you've been making excuses this whole time, it's time to examine those excuses and determine if they are actually valid.

PART 2

ON THE JOB

If you work a 40-hour workweek, you spend over 24% of each week at your job. I recognized a wonderful opportunity to improve social and mental aspects of myself at work. How you treat yourself and others at work affects how you treat yourself and others in other environments. How you respond to what happens at work affects how you respond to other life experiences. While you may not find many family or true friends on the job site, you must recognize your "work family", and I submit to you that the amount of time we spend at work and the amount of interaction we engage in at the job site make it an excellent learning laboratory.

147

CHAPTER 1: The Grounds of Struggle

Have you ever felt like it only took a second for life to get turned upside down? Sometimes it feels like life is slipping away quickly when we trip on what we perceive to be a failure. That is exactly how I felt when I did not receive a certain military promotion when I thought I should have.

The individual in control of whether I got the promotion decided to decline to respond for what seemed to be inappropriate reasoning. In the moments after I was notified of this decision, I was very emotional and even irate.

After a few days passed, I was able to put the situation into perspective. A great friend of mine, Nicole, had always advised me to not get too upset over these things – to be patient and wait for the good. I proceeded with seeking a new job and was accepted into a new position.

As it turned out, unbeknownst to me, my prior position was being eliminated and I would have had to find a new position regardless. Now I was ahead of that occurring, and although the decision of the first leader cost me one year for a future promotion, when I did get promoted, it was still six months earlier than the normal promotion timeline and for this I was grateful.

I also learned later that things are rarely, if ever, how they appear to be. Our perspectives and knowledge are always limited. Therefore, we have to be cautious of proceeding too confidently when we lack all the facts. If we charge ahead in such a situation, we will be confronted with the difficult truth and will have burned many bridges in the process.

If you are going through a struggle, take the advice of my friend and CEO of Mutt Sauce, Charlynda Nyenke Scales:

When you have a bad day, you gotta tell yourself, it is just a day. Not your life. Just a day. And soon, it will be tomorrow. Boom! New start!

Do not despair. Instead, fight the battles in front of you. Look them in the eye. Do not freeze, step in front of them, or try to frantically avoid them. Proceed in a timely manner through them with internal positivity and optimism. Rosa Luxemburg said, "Those who do not move do not notice their chains". When you engage the struggle, you can accomplish the change!

Dreams can materialize in a way we had not pictured – the key is to recognize this and remain optimistic.

— Bhakti Mary —

Imagine that you are a caterpillar. The situation you are in right now is your cocoon. You are surrounded by butterflies. You wish someone would just let you out of your situation. Well if they do, you will never become that beautiful butterfly. You need the experience of breaking the cocoon apart and beating your wings against the cocoon walls until your wings are strong enough.

The truth is that you must struggle. You are supposed to. Do you think you can reach the top if you cease climbing?

The grounds of struggle are the grounds of growth. Through struggling, you develop the abilities that you need to achieve your dreams and you move in the direction that helps you overcome the very things that have been holding you back from realizing your true potential. When you reach your dreams, do not be afraid to go beyond them!

CHAPTER 2: Becoming an Early Riser

Growing up, I was expected to rise very early, sometimes as early as 4:30 a.m. My father, Michael Beloved, has practiced yoga for over 30 years and always said that this was the most auspicious time to meditate due to the alignment between the sun and the Earth as well as the quietness of the world. My family would do yoga, meditation, and chant kirtans to Hindu gods. I never thought about what it would be like to sleep in because I did not know that "sleeping in" was a thing!

At the age of 18, I joined the military and, as you can imagine, waking up early was mandatory. Habitually, I have always been one to wake up early and get the day started whether I am feeling tired or rested. The problem is that I am both an early riser (by necessity) and a night owl (by choice/habit). I average 6-7 hours of sleep per night and over the years, the lack of sleep has worn on my body. I have tried to improve this habit by getting to sleep earlier because, to me, if

I am sleeping in, the day is wasting away and I am not accomplishing anything! Thomas Jefferson once said, "The sun has not caught me in bed in fifty years."

Rising early can lead to increased productivity. In the morning, your mind is often fresh and the world is very quiet. You have an opportunity (without rushing) to plan your day or to just think quietly which can reduce your stress or improve your response to stress as the day unfolds.

Starting your day with proactive
intention allows you to focus on what
is important instead of reacting
impulsively.

— Bhakti Mary —

Do you habitually hit the snooze button or ignore your alarm altogether? Do you wish you had more time for yourself in the morning and evenings (we ALL do)? Do you wake up at the first alarm but feel tired and exhausted (that's me!)? Here are some simple tips to help you turn around your sleep patterns:

GOAL: Set a target wake up time and a target sleep time.

ACTION: Go to bed earlier. Turn off all electronic devices 30 minutes before the target sleep time. Read a book until you start to feel tired. Then go to bed.

ACTION: Gradually wake up earlier. Try waking up 15 minutes earlier than you usually do this week. Next week make it 30 minutes and continue until you reach your target.

ACTION: Put your alarm clock far from your bed. When you get up to turn it off, stay up. Be disciplined and committed. Do you have it in you?

ACCOUNTABILITY: Find an accountability partner. For most, it may be a spouse, partner, or close friend. Commit to listening to them when they encourage you to stay on track. Be strong. Do not fall back into your old habits.

REWARD: Decide what to do with the extra time. Perhaps you will get to work earlier so you can get off earlier and spend more time with friends and family. Perhaps you will work out. Perhaps you will finally start preparing and eating a good breakfast. Perhaps you will have a few extra minutes to meditate.

CHAPTER 3: Do You Prepare for Luck?

Louis Pasteur, the inventor of Pasteurization and discoverer of the Rabies vaccine, said in the 1800s that "chance favored the prepared mind". Do you believe in luck? Does everyone recognize luck when it shows up? Do you think that people who are not prepared just fall into good opportunities and emerge successful? Why do some lucky moments ultimately lead to some of the greatest failures? How many lottery winners end up poor down the road?

Sometimes life can feel so busy that we never seem to be able to fully prepare for anything. Perhaps, the ability to properly prepare is a lost art in this world of multi-tasking. We never stop long enough to focus on much. We spend more time just "winging it" as we enter meetings or encounters throughout the day whether it be with our co-workers, our spouses, children or friends.

Sometimes we see people who have remarkable personal and professional achievements and hear people say that they just got lucky or they knew the right people. It is more likely that people's achievements are a result of being prepared and working hard. People who are prepared demonstrate a consistent sense of commitment, ownership, and pride in everything they do. When opportunities come, they are able to recognize them and take advantage because they have been preparing all along and are deserving.

The art of preparation is a fruitful practice.

— Bhakti Mary —

When luck shows up (you do not find it...it finds you!), and it rarely does, the prepared person is in the best position to seize the opportunity and generate a positive return. Put in the hard work and be patient and diligent in your preparation. Even if the results are not materializing immediately, trust that the outcome will be positive. Know that the efforts you are putting forth will prepare you for the moments you cannot imagine. We cannot predict the future, but we can humbly use the present moment to prepare for our lucky opportunity.

CHAPTER 4: Curbing Monday Morning Blues

Dear Monday,

I greatly dislike you!

Sincerely,

The World

I think that short letter appropriately describes most of my colleagues' facial expressions before 11 am on Monday morning. Do you always get the "Monday Morning Blues"? After a nice relaxing weekend, it can be hard to wake up on Monday morning. Monday morning always seems to arrive too soon, does it not? You think to yourself, "ugh...the weekend is over...". You lack passion and motivation, and you feel sluggish, anxious, sad, and even stressed out. Well you are not alone. Research shows that most workers do not smile until 11:16 am on Monday, the majority of sick leave is taken on Monday, and suicides are more likely to occur on Mondays.

Life is too short to spend any day feeling negative and the good news is that you can take deliberate steps to minimize your negative days.

— Bhakti Mary —

Here are five ways to help you turn Monday into the best day of the week.

1. GET FOCUSED. What you do each day matters. Try three techniques to get you through the Friday-Saturday-Sunday-Monday stretch. First, do not "check out" at noon on Friday. When you do this, you leave Friday's work for yourself on Monday. Second, plan out Monday's work on Friday. When you get into work on Monday, you will feel less overwhelmed and more organized. Finally, what you do on the weekend matters. Deliberately pick a day to stay at home on the weekend. Too much time out results in less sleep.

2) RISE AND SHINE. Stop being lazy and get out of bed! While it is easy to just sleep in, try to retain the same sleep schedule throughout the week for a consistent refreshed and energized

feeling. Avoid going into the weekend with a sleep deficit. If you need to, choose one weekend day to sleep in. Choosing both Saturday and Sunday can make it difficult to get back to a regular sleep schedule during the week.

3) USE SUNDAY NIGHT WISELY. Plan to get seven to nine hours of sleep. This way when your alarm clock rings, you are not likely to hit the snooze button. Set out your Monday morning outfit (make Monday your "look amazing" day – when you look great, you feel great!) and get your lunch ready in the refrigerator. When you wake up, plan to get out of the door with little stress. Then when you get to work, you can jump right into the organized list you made for yourself on Friday.

4) EAT, DRINK, AND EXERCISE RIGHT. Start the day off right! Exercising after you wake up will get your energy flowing for a productive day. I like Fitness Blender workouts – free and flexible. If you can, exercise outdoors to reduce your melatonin levels. After you exercise, give yourself

a metabolism boost by eating a healthy breakfast. As always, maximize your water intake. Do not drink alcohol excessively on the weekend. It is commonly known that alcohol is a depressant and your mood and sleep will improve if you can reduce consumption. Likewise, avoid energy drinks and caffeine after the morning hours so that you can get quality sleep. Another tip is to detach from the desk. Take 5 minutes each hour to get up and walk around. Avoid eating lunch at your desk.

5) LOOK FORWARD TO EVERY DAY. Most people always go through the work week looking forward to Friday. Live for each day. Plan fun events and spend quality time with friends and family during the week too. Be deliberate and schedule it if you have to. Still need a little extra to get through Monday? Make Monday rewarding by waking up early on Monday and heading out to your favorite spot for a quick breakfast with a friend. Or, plan something after work on Monday so you have something to look forward to.

It's time to change how you think. See Monday as a new beginning, not an end. Think of Monday as the beginning of a great week ahead instead of the end to an awesome weekend. Set your intention. Tell yourself on Sunday night that you are going to have a great day on Monday. Wake yourself up with positive affirmations. Be grateful for being alive and healthy on Monday and be grateful that you get to go to work.

CHAPTER 5: Increase Your Productivity With Melody

Trying to get some work done? Trying to relax? Distracted by all the noises around you or by your wandering mind?

I am constantly having difficulty focusing at work with all the side discussions and other distractions. Working for the federal government, I remember a time when the budget was plentiful and most people were traveling but when the budget tightened, everyone was in the office and it seemed like a different and loud conversation was always occurring at each desk. Listening to music helps me escape to a more positive present moment. Melodious sounds encourage the release of dopamine in the reward area of the brain. Dopamine is a chemical released by the ventral striatum causing a "feel good" response in the bloodstream. Discover your optimal LIFE soundtrack.

Over many years, I found that listening to music can improve my attention and memory, improve my mood, and alleviate anxiety. Instrumental music can increase concentration and productivity. Music helps me relax my mind, block outside distractions, and get organized mentally. When listening to music, I can focus on working, and I can be positively responsive to stress. Whether you want to get through a boring or tedious task or focus creatively, try listening to music while you work or relax.

CHAPTER 6: Global Leadership/Followership Staple

Are good leaders and good managers compassionate? Is good leadership and management ultimately an 'act of compassion' or 'love in action'? Is the responsible use of power compassionate? Is compassion the glue of humanity?

The Dalai Lama says that "Every human being has the same potential for compassion; the only question is whether we really take any care of that potential, and develop and implement it in our daily life." He defines compassion as "a mental attitude based on the wish for others to be free of their suffering, associated with a sense of commitment, responsibility and respect towards the other...". The Dalai Lama goes further to state that "True compassion toward others does not change even if they behave negatively. (It) is based not on our own projections and expectations, but on the needs of the other, irrespective of whether another person is a close friend or an enemy."

Tibetan scholar Thupten Jinpa defines compassion as "a mental state endowed with a sense of concern for the suffering of others and aspiration to see that suffering relieved". He details three components:

1. the cognitive component of "I understand you",

2. the affective component of "I feel for you", and

3. the motivational component of "I want to help you".

I do believe that the universal religion is compassion, and that compassion can make one an effective leader. In leadership roles, leaders are charged with shifting from an "I" mentality to a "We" perspective. Chade-Meng Tan says that great companies have compassionate leaders. There is a general sense amongst followers that humble leaders focus on the greater good for everyone instead of individual needs and wants. By understanding and feeling for others, a leader can then develop the want within to help others. A great leader will empathize with (feel for another) and feel compassion for the people he is fortunate to lead, before connecting with them and giving directives. Putting others needs before our own without expecting something in return (giving selflessly) is benevolent.

Christina Boedker, a lecturer in accounting at the Australian School of Business, says that it is critical "to understand people's motivators, hopes and difficulties and to create the right support mechanism to allow people to be as good as they can be". Geoff Aigner, director of Social Leadership Australia, believes that to activate compassionate leadership, managers need to first understand themselves and the power they exercise. Then, in an act of compassion, managers and leaders take responsibility for the growth and development of others. Compassion does not always equate to kindness, and compassion means getting people where they want to go; this can sometimes mean that a difficult conversation or decision must be conducted.

Camille Funk, an educator and author, states that "a wise leader uses compassion to perceive the needs of those he leads, and astutely determine the course of action that would be of greatest benefit to the individual as well as the team".

I believe that compassion is the global leadership and followership staple for all people in all endeavors. Everyone can embody living in self by practicing compassion – it is through this practice that one will reach a high level of existence where we truly understand the people we are charged to lead and become a part of unlocking their potential. Daren Blonski, a leadership consultant, says that "the highest and most noble form of leadership is only realized when compassion is the major operating paradigm". Throughout history, some of the world's greatest leaders were compassionate.

Great leaders envision the world in different ways and communicate their vision in a manner which resonates with people and speaks to human needs and desires in ways that

*cause mobilization towards common
goals for the greater good.*

— Bhakti Mary —

Being a compassionate person and leader can turn your routine day-to-day interactions with people into high-performance, high-engagement associations. Our relationships are our biggest assets. Here are five ways to be a compassionate leader:

1. BE PRESENT. Be aware of what is happening around you. Be mindful of the effect your words and actions are having on people in the present. Take time to listen to others and give your full attention to others. Take the time to understand others and learn what makes them tick. Make sure you are notified when people in your organization are facing hardships. Respond to this notification in the present with compassion. Acknowledge acts of compassion.

2. BE EMOTIONAL. Manage and express (not suppress) your emotions and engage in benevolent interactions. In this benevolence, do

not use judgments or criticisms as motivators. Assume the best in others.

3. BE TRANSPARENT AND OPEN. Communicate with transparency. Be transparent in your actions. Allow others to learn from your example.

4. BE FLEXIBLE AND ADAPTABLE. Be human. Care. Genuinely care. Do things for the greater good instead of always following a template. Focus on what can be done rather than blaming others.

5. BE THE EXAMPLE. Get in the trenches. Demonstrate the traits you want to see in others. You are a mirror. Look in the mirror rather than out the window. Help others – go the extra mile and do the unexpected.

CHAPTER 7: Secret Inspirers

Who inspires you? This is an important question to ask yourself. You have to find people who inspire you to be better and then take action to be better. Just like we can have secret admirers, we can have secret inspirers.

In 2014, I changed jobs and one of my first assignments on the new job was to plan the farewell for the person responsible for hiring me, Barb. Barb was in our organization for 15 years, and a large farewell was appropriate. On the day of her farewell, I listened to everyone speak about the things they would remember about her and I began to reflect on what I liked about her so much.

After 4 years, I realized why I liked Barb: She was an intelligent, hard-working, caring, and fun leader with a purpose. I had never told her openly that she inspired me. Here are five lessons I learned from my secret inspirer.

ALWAYS WORK HARD. Thomas Jefferson said, "Determine never to be idle. No person will have occasion to complain of the want of time, who never loses any. It is wonderful how much may be done, if we are always doing." Barb's accomplishments were no mistake. She was always doing. I never saw her being lazy. Hard working was her natural state. In fact, she enjoyed a challenge. Someone once told me that to abandon challenges is to abandon character development. I never saw Barb abandon challenges. She also never let people who worked for her abandon opportunities to be challenged. She walked with people through the hallways of their own challenges and when the light shone on them, those people were ready and succeeded every time. There were no chances to lazily avoid responsibility.

WORK INTELLIGENTLY. Whenever there was a chance or window to improve a process, Barb was the #1 advocate. She wasn't closed minded to change and common sense. Everything Barb asked someone to do was aligned with a desired result. Bill Bowerman said "The idea that the harder you work, the better you're going to be is just garbage. The greatest improvement is made by the man or woman who works most intelligently. You cannot succeed by working hard – you have to work harder and smarter!

VALUE TIME. Barb did not believe in pointless busywork. I do not either. When we worked, we worked hard and smart. Barb was action and goal oriented. Because she recognized that life was a balancing act, she was disciplined in the use of time. She respected her time and demonstrated regularly that she valued the time of the people she led.

In all our deeds, the proper value and respect for time determines success or failure.

— Malcom X —

HAVE FUN. We have all said "Work hard, play hard". Play is the best when you have earned it. When Barb played, we all played and we knew with certainty that we had earned it. It's like John Lubbock said, "The idle man does not know what it is to enjoy rest, for he has not earned it."

CARE ABOUT OTHERS. Barb cared about others. Because she loved herself, she was able to fully tap into her purpose. She was dedicated, committed and passionate about her work because she cared about other people. Her work mattered. People mattered. It is important to pay attention to relationships and feelings and leverage this to change individual behavior so that people can attain their greatest potential. Barb also knew what made us happy – the ability to achieve, the recognition following the achievements, the job we did, the responsibility she trusted us with, and the promotions she was able to give. At her farewell when asked what her favorite moments were, she cited hiring and recognizing people.

I began to think about my friends and co-workers that I had gravitated towards over the years, and I realized that they have all of these things in common. I am grateful for the friends, family, and leaders that surround me and teach me.

CHAPTER 8: Become a Leading Catalyst for Peace

You can pick your friends, but you cannot always pick your colleagues. You spend more waking hours at work than anywhere else, and you often rely on your colleagues to help you do your job well. At work, people of different characters and behavior meet, generating a multitude of emotions within us; then there is our own baggage.

Do you lose hours of productivity each week? Do you operate in states of chaos at work? Are you distracted by the phone calls, social media, and emails at work? Do your own thoughts distract you? There is a reason people look forward to their vacations – a place/time where/when they feel they can get away. We should not have to always wait for that annual vacation to achieve peace!

You can learn to gain inner peace and enjoy every moment, right where you are. You can stop fretting and getting tense. You can experience peace of mind and happiness wherever you are.

Peace is not something you wish for. It's something you make, something you do, something you are, and something you give away.

— Robert Fulghum —

Let us become intentional about creating order and peace at work. Cultivating a peaceful environment requires a lot of work but once you gain inner peace, you will notice your environment starting to change too. Here are 12 suggestions to help you experience and achieve inner peace at work:

1. LOOK INSIDE. Quit looking around! Stop analyzing and thinking about people's motives and behavior; focus on improving your actions. Your mother taught you the Golden Rule, didn't she? It starts with: "Do onto"...you take the first step!

2. CREATE A DAILY MORNING ROUTINE. Get up early enough that you have time to take care of yourself (quiet time, breakfast, exercise) and leave your living area in a way that you won't

dread coming home to. Each day as you walk from your car to your desk, repeat a positive affirmation. When you arrive at work, acknowledge your co-workers with a cheerful hello and smile and grab a glass of water (or something healthy) before starting your work. Let others know that you notice them and appreciate them.

3. GET FOCUSED FROM THE BEGINNING. When you arrive at your office, do not turn on your computer and open your email right away. Instead, sit down with a list of what you need to accomplish. Mark and schedule your top priorities for that day. Do not let other people's emergencies throughout the day distract you unless it is legitimate. Learn to recognize what can wait. In the military, I remember a common saying – Piss poor planning on your part does not constitute an emergency on my part. Respect your time and the time of others!

4. BE POLITE AND RESPECTFUL. Spread your good attitude. People unconsciously emulate the

behavior around them, and emotions are certainly contagious. Pretend a 4 year old is watching you. You must maintain good manners. Always work at least as hard as anyone working with or for you. Make it clear that you would never ask anyone to do a level of work you wouldn't be willing to take on yourself. When I attended the Air Force Academy, we made a habit of never asking a basic cadet to do any physical activity that we could not do ourselves. When we asked them to do something, we got in the trenches and did it with them at least once. They respected us a lot more as a result. Another element of respect is timeliness. Always be on time to show you respect other people's time.

5. CONTROL YOURSELF. Whenever you feel tension or anger building in you, take some deep slow breaths before any talking or action. Pay attention to your mind and spirit. When you find yourself getting "passionate", lower your voice, Focus on using positive words in writing and speech.

6. TAKE BREAKS. Walk away from your desk and get a breath of fresh air or a cup of water periodically. Do not neglect your body's need for exercise and nutrition. I had a colleague who would ask me if I needed to take a walk to the coffee shop when he noticed that I seemed to be getting stressed out at my desk. After the walk was over, I always felt a sense of relief. Now I do the same for my colleagues.

7. TALK TO AND WITH (NOT ABOUT) PEOPLE. People love to be asked their opinion, so go out of your way to ask what they think. I always remember Oprah saying that all people want to be heard...we all just want to be heard. Be heard in a positive way. Express your good ideas in a way that makes it clear that they are not the only good ideas; recognize and make it apparent that you believe others may have equally good insights to add. And when they're talking, listen intently. Retain the trust and respect of your colleagues by not being known as the office enquirer or gossiper.

8. CREATE COMFORT. Declutter your physical space. Make your work environment an efficient one. Get rid of old books & materials that can easily be found online and items you no longer need. Make room for items you use regularly. Keep a personal photo or two at your desk to remind you of home and loved ones.

9. RECOGNIZE PEOPLE. Do not withhold credit from deserving colleagues. Be the first to acknowledge excellent performance. When you are incorrectly recognized, direct the attention to the colleagues who do deserve the credit. Recognize the small and big achievements. They are all important on some level.

10. BE HUMAN. Talk with your co-workers about your life outside the office when it's appropriate as a reminder of the humanity factor. At the end of the day, we are all human with basic wants and needs that are sometimes facilitated by the money we earn at work. Showing a genuine interest in people will make them feel comfortable around you. And, it's the right thing

to do. Trust me when I say that your colleagues know who genuinely cares about them.

11. BE POSITIVE. Assume the positive about what you do not know. For example, at my job we always seem to be talking about how our bosses do not know what's going on or that another site does not seem to be working hard. While the results sometimes seem to indicate these things, they still may be untrue and no one benefits from the negative thinking or portrayal. Also do not be the "party of no" at work. Stop finding ways not to do work and ways that success cannot be achieved; be creative and bring fresh ideas to the table instead of the stale cynicism that plagues many organizations.

12. DISCONNECT FROM THE RESULTS. This is probably the most controversial of my suggestions. I believe if you can disconnect from the outcome of your work, you can be happier just knowing that you did your best. If you did your best, then you can learn to do better next time if the outcome was undesired. You cannot give

more than 100%. Sometimes even when you give all you have, it is still not enough for some people, but it has to be enough for you. Even if the outcome is not as expected, you have to disconnect from wanting the outcome to be different. It is what it is and there's no need to beat yourself up over it. Free up your mind to tap into creative spaces the next time around!

CHAPTER 9: Doing the Work

In 2015, Kendall Schler, who was originally declared the winner of the 2015 St. Louis Marathon on April 12, had her title taken away and was officially disqualified after marathon officials discovered that she cheated to win the race. Schler came onto the course at the last checkpoint to cross the finish line before the other 582 female runners. During the race, she was never seen among competitors or among the leaders. She certainly is not the only runner to take a shortcut during a marathon!

There is no quick road to success and there are no huge shortcuts. When you are on a long journey, a shortcut can be very tempting. The motivation that over 500,000 runners complete marathons each year through honest hard work is not enough for some who want to receive recognition that they did not earn.

Prepare yourself along your journey for success. Create your own definition of success by defining milestones that result from your hard work.

Mingle with competitors and even with leaders when the opportunities present themselves. View their company as a learning opportunity, a motivational moment, or an encouraging encounter. Keep trying...and when you finally cross the finish line, you will be recognized as a deserving recipient.

brownBerry Books

A collection of books named after some of the most beautiful flowers in the world that reflect Bhakti Mary's thoughts regarding her self-improvement as she experienced life. The brownBerry book series focuses on current well-being and preparation for a lifetime of abundant joy through sustained social, mental, and physical fitness.

The views and opinions expressed are solely hers. She encourages you to have brownBerry thoughts or discussions where you take a situation and cultivate learning by exploring its application to your self-improvement journey. We can learn much from what is happening to us and around us.

Online Resources

Email: brownberrybooks@gmail.com

Website: brownberrybooks.com

Forum: liveinself.com